The Photographer's Computer Handbook

THE PHOTOGRAPHER'S COMPUTER HANDBOOK

B. Nadine Orabona

Writer's Digest Books

Cincinnati, Ohio

 Published by Writer's Digest Books, 9933 Alliance Road, Cincinnati, Ohio 45242. First edition.

Library of Congress Cataloging in Publication Data

Orabona, Nadine, 1940-
The photographer's computer handbook.

Includes index.
1. Photography—Business methods—Data processing. I. Title.
TR581.'72 1984 770'.68 84-17215
ISBN 0-89879-150-2

Book design by Joan Ann Jacobus.

To MAC

for his tireless help, patience, and persistence;
for teaching me a great deal about microcomputers;
for making writing this book a lot easier.

(MAC is my MAChine, my Kaypro II computer.)

Acknowledgments

I was most fortunate to have a very knowledgeable and helpful computer salesperson, and I would like to thank Max J. Rochlin for all his help and assistance and for reading this book to make sure my technical information was correct.

I would also like to thank my editor at Writer's Digest Books, Robert D. Lutz, for taking such a personal interest in my book and making many helpful suggestions. He made producing the final version a very easy task.

And finally, I would like to thank Carol Leigh Cardwell for the long hours she put into reading and editing the early versions of the book. As a photographer interested in using a computer in her work, she was able to guide my writing so it was directed at the proper level—to you, the photographer.

Contents

1

ENTER THE COMPUTER AGE

The computer has entered your life—and things will never be the same. You suddenly find yourself learning a new vocabulary and facing the computer everywhere you turn. When you check out books at the library, the computer records your choices. You make an airline reservation, and the computer works out all the details. A trip to the market finds a computer scanning a bar code on your selected items to record the prices and to provide a detailed list of your purchases. A computer dispenses money at the bank. The computer in your car may talk back to you to warn you that the car is low on gas. And yes, even your camera is computerized to make precisely correct exposures, to control your flash, and to focus your lens.

There are more computers in your life than you probably realize. The microwave oven that cooks your dinner is a computer that follows your "programmed" instructions. The thermostat controlling your heat is another computer that follows your settings. The videotape recorder, your electronic calculator, and, of course, those electronic games are all computers, as well as that digital watch that tells you more about time than you care to know. Computers are everywhere.

All the computers mentioned above are *special-purpose* computers. That is, they are designed to perform a simple, well-defined task. Now enters the *personal computer.* Unlike the other computers with which you've had contact, this is a *general-purpose* computer, one designed to perform a variety of tasks. These tasks are defined for the computer by instructions that tell it what to do. When you want the computer to do a new task, you change to a new set of instructions. These instructions are called *software.* But even the software is generalized.

Your business requirements may be similar to, but still very different from, those of an accountant, an insurance agent, or even another photographer. Generalized machines and software allow you to design a customized system for your particular business, but at the same time, you must put in a lot more effort than you had to when you were just setting your microwave oven. You must specifically define the task you want done on the computer; the software will help you, but you are the one who must make it work. This book is designed to help you develop your own systems for your photographic business.

But the first question to be asked is: Do you really need a computer?

Why should a photographer care about computers? You take great pictures with your manual camera and still remember filter factors. You can add up a column of figures without a pocket calculator. You know it's Wednesday without help from your digital watch. And you still use carbon paper so you don't have to run down to the photocopy machine every day. But let's look at this scenario.

1.1 A TALE OF TWO PHOTOGRAPHERS

Enter two photographers. Both are freelance stock photographers and handle all their own clerical work. They have both just returned from a trip to Australia where they've been taking pictures to build up their stock files. It's just about tax time, so they also have to get their income and expense records together for their accountants. The only difference is that the first photographer, Bob, is doing business in the old way—without a computer—while the second, Carol, is using her personal computer. Each task performed by Bob would probably take a full day, while Carol, with a computer, could probably accomplish each task in about an hour.

First Photographer

Day 1:
Bob took three thousand slides during his stay in Australia. They all must be captioned before they can be filed away. He has at least two hundred terrific pictures of kangaroos, but printing "Great Gray Kangaroo, *Macropus giganteus*" two hundred times on his slide mounts reminds him of grade school punishment. After that there are about one hundred of "Opera House, Sydney, Australia," and so on. It takes most of the day and his patience, but the job has to be done.

Day 2:
With all these new slides, it's time for Bob to update his stock list. He makes a list of all the subjects in his files and then spends several hours alphabetizing it. Since it must all fit on one page, the list will require three typed columns. Bob works it all out and types up the list. When finished, he realizes that the last column has three items too many, so he has to retype the whole list. Finally finished, he discovers that somehow he forgot the kangaroos.

Day 3:
Today Bob decides to mail his new stock list to prospective clients. He pulls out his index cards to type up a letter, an envelope, and a label for a return postcard for each client. At the end of a very long day, about thirty clients are done.

Day 4:
A lot of mail accumulated while he was gone. There are quite a few clients who want pictures. One client is looking for apple blossoms. Bob remembers he has some great apple blossom pictures but can't seem to find them in any of his flower categories. After hours of searching, he locates them under "Yosemite National Park," where he had taken the photographs.

Each client requires a personal letter and a form that spells out the terms of submission. Bob has photocopied his "Terms of Submission," so that part is easy. Only one client requests permission to hold the pictures sixty days instead of the thirty days Bob has specified, so that form has to be retyped. Also, he has been meaning to update some of the items on his price list. He only wants to make a couple of changes, but it means retyping the whole thing.

Day 5:
While Bob was out of town, a backlog of follow-up work has accumulated. He goes through his index cards again and discovers that several clients have been holding pictures for more than thirty days, so he must get letters out to them. One client hasn't paid a bill, so he must send out a reminder. The day's mail has a letter from a client indicating that he wants to use some pictures, so Bob now has to prepare an invoice.

Day 6:
Bob is also a writer. He had started an article before leaving for Australia; now he wants to get it finished and in the mail. It's been revised and retyped several times, cut up and pasted together, and needs a final typed copy. After typing the whole thing, he decides that it would really be better if he had led off with the last paragraph, and that the middle section just doesn't work and should be deleted. He revises it again and retypes it. Bob is a poor speller, so he takes the time to look up all the words he questions. He is suspicious of "percise" but can't seem to find it in the dictionary.

Finally, he's finished. He rereads it. One or two sentences could be better, but he figures he will just let it go.

Day 7:
Today is the day Bob has set aside to get last year's books in order. He must get all of last year's income and expense figures together for his accountant. Bob sits down with his adding machine to total up all of last year's figures, writing them out for his accountant. He discovers that he earned more money last year than he had expected, and now wishes he had purchased that new camera in December instead of January, which would have allowed a bigger deduction against last year's income.

Late that evening, when everything is done, Bob wonders when he will ever find time to do some more photography.

Second Photographer

9:00 a.m.:
Carol also took three thousand pictures on her Australian trip. She sits down at her computer and enters:

KANGAROO, Great Gray
Macropus giganteus
200

And the printer runs off two hundred half-inch labels in a neat, compressed print. She does this with each subject, and within the hour, all her slides are professionally labeled.

10:00 a.m.:
With all those new slides, Carol also decides she should update her stock list. She enters the new categories into her stock file database. Then she indicates on her computer that she wants to select only those categories with twenty or more slides and wants them to be sorted alphabetically and printed on a single sheet of paper. A few minutes later, a neatly typed stock list comes off the printer.

11:00 a.m.:
Carol is anxious to get her stock list in the mail and out to prospective clients. She sits down with her word processor and puts together a form letter pointing out all the new Australian additions. She runs a form letter against the client database. Out come personalized letters addressed to all her clients, followed by addressed envelopes and mailing labels for the postcards.

12:00 noon:
Carol takes a quick lunch break. Then she goes back to the computer and dials up the computer network on the telephone. (The computer network is a large computer where many photographers and picture buyers can communicate their pictures, availability, and needs to each other.) She checks the posted picture needs and finds several publishers who are interested in

Australia. While she is on-line, she posts a notice on the electronic bulletin board, indicating that she has just returned from Australia with many new pictures.

Through the network, Carol has established contact with several photographers throughout the country. They exchange photo leads. She had sent messages to all her contacts, telling them about her Australian trip. Her electronic mailbox has a message from a sports photographer, who knows of a publisher who is doing a book on marsupials and is looking for pictures of kangaroos.

1:00 p.m.:
Since she is going to be pulling pictures, Carol also searches the accumulated mail for picture requests. There is one request for apple blossoms. She goes back to the computer and checks "apple blossoms" against her stock file database; "apple blossoms" is cross-referenced to "Yosemite."

Carol already has standard form letters in the system for submitting pictures and stating the terms of submission. All she has to do is pull off the addresses from her client database. While she is at it, Carol brings up her price list on the word processor, makes a few changes, and prints a new price list to include with the submissions. Since one client wants to hold the pictures sixty days instead of thirty days, she changes the "thirty days" to "sixty days" before she prints the "Terms of Submission" for that client.

2:00 p.m.:
Since she has been out of town for several weeks, Carol decides to check for any past-due items. Her query to the client database reveals several clients who have had pictures for more than thirty days, plus one client who has not paid his bill. Since she already has form letters for these situations, she merely selects the appropriate letter; the computer pulls the names and addresses from the client database and prints the letters and envelopes. While she is at the computer, Carol also prints a standard invoice for a client who wants to use some of her pictures.

3:00 p.m.:
With the day's work done, it is time for Carol to get back to that article she has been writing. She brings it up on her word processor. There are several paragraphs she wants to rearrange, which she can do with ease since she is only moving the text around in the computer's memory. She makes some other revisions, then runs the text through the spelling checker, which picks up many typing errors and questions the spelling of "percise." Carol instructs the spelling checker to look up the correct spelling. It comes back with the spelling "precise" and makes the correction in the text wherever the word appears. Finally, she prints the article and settles back to read it. A couple of sentences really should be changed, so she just makes the changes and reprints the article.

4:00 p.m.:
It is time for Carol to gather for her accountant her figures for last year's income and expenses. She sits down again at the computer to print out last year's figures from her accounting spreadsheet. It is worked out neatly with everything totaled. In fact, everything is already posted to the proper tax lines on the proper tax forms and added up there, too. Why does she need an accountant? She is also glad her income and expenses are always up-to-date. She might have otherwise waited until January before buying that new camera.

The end of the day—and a good day's work. Now that she has all the clerical work out of the way, Carol can get out and take more pictures.

1.2

SURVIVING THE COMPUTER AGE

It is quite obvious that Carol has some advantages over Bob. She can accomplish in a day what takes Bob a week to do. Not only is the computer a time-saver, allowing Carol time to go out and build more stock, but she can do a lot more. She can go through directories for the names and addresses of hundreds or even thousands of potential picture buyers, put them on her client file, and send to them her stock list. Every few months she can send them updated stock lists. Since all the names and addresses are already in her computer file, this will require very little work. If either photographer suddenly has hundreds of people wanting pictures, Bob will have a hard time keeping up, while Carol will have little difficulty.

These two photographers happen to be stock photographers, but all types of photographers can benefit from a computer. If you are primarily a photographer/writer, the computer can help you turn out prose in one third of the time, in addition to checking your spelling and punctuation. A whole library of research material is available to you instantly from the many computer networks. If you are a wedding or portrait photographer, or if you work on an assignment basis, the computer can keep your busy schedule current as well as handle your routine business work. Through the networks, you can find assignments anywhere in the world and advertise your availability for them. Even technical data can be stored in your computer so that they are instantly available whenever you need them.

A computer is not just a nice thing to have. In the future it will be the only way to survive. In a volume business, the nonautomated photographer cannot possibly compete with the automated one. Having a computer will allow you to reach more clients, do so on a more timely basis, make more sales and money, help you keep control of your business, give you a more professional appearance, and, most of all, leave you more free time for photography.

You are convinced. So where do you go to sign up and get started with this little wonder? Not so fast—before you ever get anything out of a computer, you have to make a big commitment to it. If your business isn't big enough, it might not be worth the time and trouble. If you just don't have the time or patience to go through the initial learning period, it may be a waste of time for you. If you don't properly plan the way you will use your computer, or if you make improper machine and software choices, then you are just wasting time and money and will never use it. This book will guide you through those decisions and show you how you can use a computer and survive—and prosper doing it.

2

APPROACHING AUTOMATION

You've heard a lot about computers. You may be a little intimidated by all the technical jargon and mystified by all the magical, wondrous things that a computer is supposed to do. You may be a little afraid to touch the computer because you think you might hurt it. You may even have some science-fiction notion that the machine possesses some sort of superhuman intelligence.

But you are interested in getting a computer to help you with your photography business. You already have some ideas of how you might be able to use it. But where do you begin? What machine should you buy? What software will you need? How do you choose among hundreds of word processing systems? How do you ever learn how to use that software? How do you make it work with your business? It can be very overwhelming.

2.1

THE DECISION-MAKING PROCESS

The process of acquiring a computer and automating your business does not start with the machine, or even with the software, but with you and your business. You have to make a commitment to the project. In spite of what some people may tell you, you don't just buy a computer and all the software you need, plug it in, and start doing business. Software development, while it is improving, has not reached a level where a totally unsophisticated user can simply sit down at a computer, conduct a friendly but informative conversation, and suddenly have everything working perfectly.

You will also discover that computer-based systems are very dumb. A computer does everything in exactly the way you instruct it. If you are not knowledgeable enough to tell it precisely the correct way to do something—and the emphasis must be on precision—the results will be at best unpredictable. So let's look at the steps you take before you go out and buy that machine.

First, you must believe that you have a need for a computer, and that it's not just a matter of keeping up with the photographer next door. The things a computer does well are simple, repetitive, easily defined tasks. It's also good at storing and retrieving massive amounts of data. If you are a weekend photographer who sells your photography just to offset your equipment costs, it is probably not worth the cost or the time. Some things are still managed better with manual systems. The keys are *volume* and *repetition*. But if you do a high-volume, through-the-mail business, keep track of thousands of pictures, do extensive follow-up activity, constantly retrieve or change information in your files, and find that you spend a considerable amount of time on these clerical activities, you should definitely consider looking into a computer system.

The second thing you will need is *commitment*. You will have to spend a lot of time learning about computer systems and software. You will have to spend time evaluating and organizing your business. You certainly will have to spend a lot of time learning to use whatever software you get. Depending upon your prior computer experience, you should expect to spend one to two weeks just getting anything going, even after you have everything together and the computer plugged in. It may be several months before you have a working and useful operation.

One often overlooked and very time-consuming task is putting all the necessary information into the computer. If you're very organized and, for instance, have all your client information on index cards, you can have someone else do it for you. If you are not, or can't find someone else to do it, you are the one who must key in all that client information.

Because of all the work involved in setting up an effective computer system, there will be times when you will wish you had never heard of computers and regret that you ever got involved with them. But just remember that the hardest part in implementing a computer system is educating the user—*you*. Most problems can be attributed to your lack of knowledge. But once you are committed to a computer system, stick with it. One of the facts of automation is that a mediocre system can be made to work and work well if you want that, while the best system in the world will fail if you lose confidence in it. Take heart. Once your system is up and running, you will overlook all the frustrations you suffered and wonder how you ever lived without a computer.

So you've decided your business could benefit from a computer; you are willing to make the commitment to make a computerized system work. The next step is to make a list of the things that you think you can computerize. This book will help you with some suggestions. Later you will organize this list in terms of your priorities and the tasks that affect your business the most. If you are a photographer/writer, word processing may be high on your list. If you spend a lot of time trying to reach hundreds of clients, a file management/mail generation system may be very important to you. If you could benefit from the services of a photographic network, going on-line may be your highest priority.

Next you should determine the quality of the organization of your present systems. If you need a computer to help you locate pictures but haven't started any filing system, you will have to develop one before you can use a computer. The same thing is true if you haven't kept track of your clients, your expenses, or the whereabouts of the pictures you've sent out. Computers like things nicely classified, with all relevant data in their appropriate boxes. I will cover the ways you can approach this in later chapters. Just keep in mind that a computer cannot help you unless you have organized and quantified the data with which it must work. Perhaps the best part about this procedure is that it will force you to become organized.

Now that you are organized, have made your list and set your priorities, it's time to look at software. Software tells your computer how to perform. Notice that I haven't even discussed hardware considerations yet, because the important thing is to select the software that is best suited for the job you want to do. Then select the machine that will run the software.

2.2

DO YOU REALLY NEED A COMPUTER?

After reading the first chapter of this book, you were probably sold. You need a computer. After reading the last section, you might not be so sure anymore. First, you have to examine your business to see if, in computer jargon, buying a computer is going to be *cost effective*. A computer is expensive, the software necessary to run the computer is expensive, it will take a lot of your time to get your system operational, and it may be cheaper to simply hire a part-time clerk. You must take a close look at the amount of work a computer can potentially do for you in terms of the expense of the system. You will also have to weigh the intangible benefits, such as the ability to reach potential clients whom you would be unable to reach without a computer.

Briefly, ask yourself the following questions:

- Do you run a business that requires you to spend a lot of your time doing routine clerical work? Is most of that work repetitive?
- Could you benefit from some of the services provided by the photography networks, such as locating assignments for you or notifying you of the picture needs of clients?
- Can you afford a computer or the services of a network in terms of the income you make in photography?
- Are your photographic activities hindered by your routine business activities?
- Do you feel you could really sell more pictures or services if you could just reach more people?
- Do you actually have some specific functions you would like the computer to perform?

Many times as you read through this book, I will come back to these points. Too many computers are purchased and never used, or are abandoned when their owners become discouraged with all the work involved in using them. Too often, owners are totally unhappy with the results of their computerized systems.

2.3

FEAR OF AUTOMATION

Ever since computers were first introduced to the business world in the 1950s, people have been afraid of them, fearing that computers would eliminate their jobs. In fact, computers have created more jobs than they've eliminated. People feared that they were uncontrollable and had "minds" of their own, and that no one could stop them. But computers turned out to be too dumb to realize their destiny.

When computers did make mistakes, they were big ones. They could quickly destroy all the records of a company. They were stubborn and unfeeling when your charge account got mixed up with that of someone else. They could even be ridiculous, persistently billing you for $0.00 amount "owed" on a bill. But these are human errors, not machine errors. Humans aren't machines, so they make mistakes. Machines are dumb and do precisely what their human programmers tell them to do.

A mystique was built around computers. They were kept in se-

...e served by elite high priests. These priests ...age that no one understood and few dared to ...ings using the information provided by the ... to that mystique. Question someone about a ...d the computer is never wrong. Inquire as to ... check and you were told the computer was ...wait until the all-knowing machine was oper- ...ld get an answer. Everyone deferred to com-

...personal." It is no longer a big, hulking ma- ...nd whirling tapes. It looks just like a cross ...iter and TV set. Your next-door neighbor ... even put film in his camera without your ... in the TV commercials don't seem to have ...ot you? But you may still be a little timid. ... When self-service gas stations became ...l-service stations and pay the extra price ...nid about using a gasoline pump. I was ...e out how it worked. A computer is a lot ...ne pump, but the problem is the same. ... able to figure out how to use one. You ...questions to ask. The salesman at the computer store doesn't help much by throwing a lot of computerese at you as soon as you walk in the door. Even the computer store itself, full of sterile machines and eager salespeople, is a little intimidating. I will cover coping with computer stores and salespeople later on. If you are timid, you just need to know a little more about how the thing works and what questions to ask.

One solution is to pick up your checkbook, march into the computer store, and purchase the computer promoted by your favorite movie star. Some people buy cameras that way, but that wasn't the way you bought your camera. Your computer and your camera are important tools for your business. You learned about cameras before you made your choice. You should do the same thing with computers.

Not long ago there was very little information about computers; now there is a great deal. Take a little time to learn about them. In fact, take all the time you need until you feel comfortable enough to ask the right questions and make the right decision. Read the books and magazines; talk to your friends who have computers. Don't be intimidated by some notion that you have to learn to program a computer. You *don't* have to learn programming to use a computer any more than you had to learn lens design to use your camera.

You can use a computer without knowing how it works. But if you do learn a little about how the computer works, you will be less intimidated by it and better able to use it in ways that will do you the most good. There are some things a computer is very good at doing and some things that it cannot do very well, if at all. You'll find lots of suggestions in this book, but recognize that each situation is unique. You'll need to customize your computer system to suit your specific business.

2.4

LEARNING ABOUT COMPUTERS AND SOFTWARE

You've bought this book and that is a good start—it will cover just about everything you'll need to know to get started with a computer system. You may want to look at other books devoted solely to computer topics. Go to the computer book section of your bookstore or library. The selection of titles may initially overwhelm you, so just browse at first. The only books you'll want to consider are those that have been in print or have been revised in the past two or three years. Things change too fast in the computer field for older books to still be relevant. Avoid specialized books on programming, or on how to use a particular type of software, or that are specialized for a specific machine. These you may want to consider later, after you have made some decisions.

Take a look at the magazines; these will be more current. Many will have articles geared to the first-time user; the magazine publisher may publish a special issue devoted to helping the beginner select his first computer or a particular type of software, like word processing. Note that some magazines may be specialized for a particular machine or type of software. Select only the general-information magazines. Read only what interests you. There is just too much information for you to follow every topic. Later on you will find yourself interested in the specific software and hardware reviews.

You can visit a computer store, talk to a salesperson, and see a demonstration of a computer and software. You probably should not go into a computer store until you know something about software and equipment. Computer stores carry limited choices in both; the salespeople are inclined to push what they have in stock. They tend to use a lot of computer jargon and may ask you a lot of questions you are not prepared to answer. Once you are comfortable with some of the jargon and have a good idea of what you are looking for, a computer store is the best place to go to get firsthand experience with a system. Don't go to just one; go to several to compare the suggestions given to you by the salespeople. Remember, they are in business to sell their products and will be biased toward those products.

Computer shows are just like photo shows—great events to attend to immerse yourself in all the new computers and software. Check the calendar sections of the magazines for the many upcoming shows. The biggest is COMDEX (COMputer Dealers EXposition). The COMDEX trade shows, held each year in Las Vegas, Los Angeles, Atlanta, Amsterdam, and Tokyo, are expanding to other cities. With more than fifteen hundred exhibits, COMDEX can be overwhelming, but you can collect a lot of brochures and, in one place, see virtually everything that is available in computers, software, and related products. Don't ignore the smaller trade shows that may come to your town. Their smaller size makes it somewhat easier for you to absorb the products on display. There is a fee for attending these shows, but you can often get free passes or discount tickets through your local computer dealer.

2.5

THE *IDIOT SAVANT*

Actually, just the word "computer" can be misleading. Most people think of a computer as a system of hardware, since it requires a *microprocessor* (the control unit) plus other support machinery to make it functional. Sometimes the word "computer" is applied to just the microprocessor. Beware of ads offering a computer at a very low price. They are probably selling just the microprocessor, which is the least expensive component in the system. As you will soon learn, a microprocessor by itself is useless to you. What you really want is a "computer system"—a combination of microprocessor, support hardware, and software. Each of these systems may be priced separately or included in a package deal.

The heart of any computer system is the microprocessor, more generally referred to as the *Central Processing Unit* (CPU). This is the powerhouse of the system, and it is all packed onto a half-inch sliver of silicon the size of your thumbnail. The microprocessor is basically a counting machine capable of moving data around and making simple comparisons of that data. That's all it can do—but it does it accurately and at incredible speeds. The computer is able to perform all its wondrous tasks by creatively utilizing those simple functions of counting, moving, and comparing done at tremendous speeds and in an extremely small package. It is similar to its human counterpart, the *idiot savant*, brilliant in his ability to manipulate numbers and perform arithmetic operations, but stupid in everything else. It has been said that our most sophisticated computers have the intelligence of a primitive insect, but even this might be too generous an assumption. As soon as you start working with a computer, you will realize that they are single-minded idiots.

Since it is a counting machine, a computer recognizes only numbers. However, the numbers a computer uses are quite different from the numbers you and I use. Because man's first counting machine was his fingers, we humans use a *decimal* system of counting. Our ten fingers give us ten counting symbols. When we reach the limit of our symbols, we indicate the next number by an additional place position and reuse our symbols. So after nine we use ten, cycling through all our symbols in all possible combinations for those two positions until they are exhausted. After reaching ninety-nine, we move over one more position again, and so on. Each progression represents a power of ten.

The computer has a lightbulb mentality and can recognize only an electrical "on" or "off" condition. The computer, essentially, has one finger. It can recognize *0* and *1*, but when it gets to *2*, it has run out of fingers and symbols. Just as when we reached the end of our fingers (0-9) and had to indicate the next number by using another place, the computer must represent the next number, *2*, as a *10*. If you follow the progression of numbers, you will notice that each time an additional place is required, the number represented is a power of two.

Actually, this seemingly irrelevant bit of knowledge will help you follow all the numbers that are thrown around in computer jargon. The

Decimal	Binary
0	0
1	1
2	10
3	11
4	100
5	101
6	110
7	111
8	1000
9	1001
10	1010
100	1100100
1000	1111011110

2-A. Decimal and Binary Number Systems

progression of powers of two are 2, 4, 8, 16, 32, 64, 128, 256, 512, and 1024. These numbers show up time and time again. Since it is based on powers of two, the computer's method of counting is called a *binary* system. The smallest unit of information represented by its single "finger" is called a *bit*, an abbreviation of *binary digit*. A bit is usually represented as a *0* or *1*.

The pure binary system is quite unmanageable. The number *1024* is represented in the computer as *10000000000*. Very large numbers become astronomically long. So bits are grouped together as units to represent individual decimal digits. Though there are many systems for representing binary numbers, using 8 bits to represent a logical element such as a letter of the alphabet or a number has become the standard. This 8-bit unit is called a *byte*.

In microcomputers, the coding scheme used to represent numbers is called *ASCII* (the *A*merican *S*tandard *C*ode for *I*nformation *I*nterchange). In this system, 7 bits (which can represent the numbers 0 to 127 in binary form) are assigned specific values or operations. Numbers 0 to 31 represent operations; number 32 through 127 are assigned to represent numbers, letters, and special characters. Note that the value of the ASCII number does not correspond to the value of the number it represents. It is just a coding system. (See Appendix A for ASCII codes.) The eighth bit is not used as part of the ASCII code system; its use varies from computer to computer.

The Central Processing Unit (CPU) can turn bits off and on with lightning speed, but it must have two other components before this function can begin to be useful. First, it must have a means of transmitting that information to other components of the system. This is usually referred to as the *I/O* (Input/Output) *interface*. It also must have *internal memory*. There are two types of memory. *Read-only memory* contains instructions that are necessary for the computer's operation. So that you will not be left out of cocktail-party conversation, it is usually referred to as *ROM*.

Sometimes computers come with considerable ROM and contain permanent programs and instruction sets in this memory. This kind of program or instruction set is usually referred to as *firmware* because it is permanently fixed into the machine. Since you really do not have access to this memory, you want to evaluate your computer only in terms of the amount of *random-access memory*, or *RAM*, it has. It is the size of the RAM that determines how much data you can work on at one time and, in many cases, what software or programs you can use in your system. The number 1024 in binary, the closest thing a computer has to 1,000, is usually referred to as *K* (for kilobyte). You will see references to computer memory as 64K, which stands for a memory capacity of roughly 64,000 characters (bytes) of information.

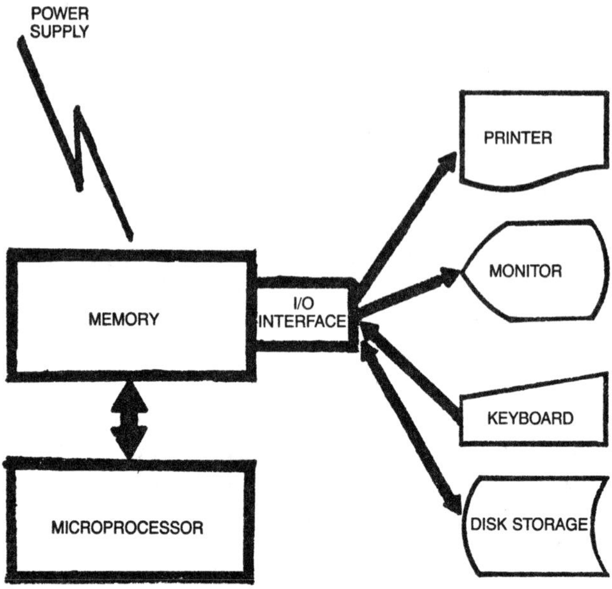

2-B. Computer Hardware System

2.6

WHAT IS SOFTWARE?

Software tells your computer what to do. Even with all the hardware in place and no software, a computer can still do nothing. It is a "brain" with nothing in it. You turn it on, and it just blinks at you or may display a cryptic message like "Put diskette in drive A." There are many types of software your system will need. These also will be covered in more detail in later chapters.

Operating System: The operating system is the most important software you will need. Think of it as the "boss" instructing all your other software "workers" in what to do. Without it, none of your other software will work. It also handles a lot of the housekeeping chores, such as keeping track of the location of your data on your disk files. Applications software, or software designed to perform a specific job function such as updating your stock file, is written to work with a specific operating system. Your choice of operating system actually determines what kind of application software you can use.

Programming Languages: Don't worry about learning programming languages unless you plan to write your own custom programs. Programming languages allow you to translate the tasks you want the computer to perform into a form the computer can understand.

Generalized Applications Software: This type of software gives you freedom to design or use your own system without having to resort to custom programming. These general applications include such areas as *word processing, file* or *data management,* and *financial management*—popularly referred to as *spreadsheets.* Word processing will help you with your correspondence, file management will take care of your filing and retrieval problems, and spreadsheets will help with your finances and bookkeeping. These will be discussed in great detail since they are the most useful for your photo business.

Specific Applications Software: Some software is designed to perform specific tasks, such as bookkeeping or tax preparation. Structured tasks, like those found in accounting, are best handled by this type of software. If you use specific applications software, you must make your business conform to the rules of the software.

2.7

WHAT IS HARDWARE?

Hardware consists of all the physical components of a computer system, including the microprocessor and the input, output, and storage devices usually called *peripherals.* Each component will be covered in detail in another chapter, but for now, you should have some idea of what you will need to make a system work. Our microprocessor now has memory and an I/O interface, but it still has no physical means of communicating with the outside world. It is very much like a brain in a glass jar with no eyes, or ears or hands or any other way to communicate. Minimally, you will need the following components to have a working system. Sometimes they can be purchased separately, but most often all, with the exception of the printer, come packaged together.

Keyboard: The keyboard looks very much like a typewriter and is your basic means of communicating with the computer. There are many different keyboard designs, but as far as letters and numbers are concerned, they are just like a standard typewriter.

Screen Monitor: The screen monitor usually looks like a TV set and, in fact, can be your TV. Most often, it is a high-resolution *CRT (cathode-ray tube)* or an *LCD (liquid-crystal display)*, similar to the type used on your digital watch. It is the primary way the computer communicates with you. It also gives you feedback on your communication to the computer.

Mass Storage Device: The computer has a limited memory capacity that is wiped clean when the computer is shut off. You must have some means of storing large amounts of data and program instructions. *Cassettes, diskettes,* and large-capacity *disks* are the common means for storing data for microcomputers. These forms of storage and the devices necessary to utilize them will be covered in detail in Chapter 5, Selecting a Computer.

Printer: A printer is an output device that transfers computer data to paper. A printer is usually sold as a separate item, but it will be an essential component of your system. It also may be the most expensive. The price can range from a few hundred dollars to several thousand dollars, depending on the speed and quality of the printer.

Basically, that is all you will need in the way of hardware. If you want to use the services of a network such as Photonet or Photo-1, you will also need a *modem*. A modem (*mo*dulator/*dem*odulator) is a device used to translate the digital data from your computer to the sound-wave form carried by your telephone lines and back again. Modems and their use will be covered in Chapter 10, The Photo Networks.

The next four chapters in this book will give you detailed help in evaluating the needs of your photo business, the types of software you will want to consider to meet those needs and how to evaluate them, and, finally, how to make your hardware selection.

3

MAKING IT WORK WITHOUT BEING A COMPUTER EXPERT

You can have a complete, computerized system designed to handle your unique photography business—and you don't even have to be a computer expert. The secret is in the software you choose to run your business. The software tells the computer how to perform specific functions. Although the first step in your decision-making process is deciding what operations in your business can be done effectively and efficiently by a computer, you must first know what a computer is capable of doing. A computer is capable of doing what the software can tell it to do. Though a little premature, a discussion of software is necessary if you are going to evaluate which business applications can be managed on a computer.

3.1

THE SOFTWARE REVOLUTION

Software has always lagged behind the capabilities of the computer hardware. In the past, most software was custom designed and written for a particular user. This was both time consuming and expensive. Software written for one person or one business was not readily usable by another, and usually required extensive modification. Some attempts were made at developing off-the-shelf software, but most of these attempts resulted in products that still had to be modified. The greatest success was in very structured areas such as accounting applications or inventory control. Even there, the user either had to conform to the rules of the software or have it modified to his own requirements.

The microcomputer revolution brought along with it a software revolution. Microcomputers were first purchased by hobbyists who enjoyed working with the technical side of computing. But when people started buying microcomputers for their homes and small businesses, they needed software to run their microcomputers, and there was very little software available. These home and business users were not up to writing their own programs, they couldn't afford to hire programmers to write the programs for them, and they needed something that was very easy to use (or "user-friendly") to help them over the technical hurdles. The machine was there—capable and affordable—and software developers were quick to realize the importance of this market.

Prior to the introduction of the microcomputer, programmers were limited to developing prescribed business systems for their employers or clients on their specific types of machines. There was little motivation to develop any software beyond that. The same was true of software houses, which mainly developed software for known clients. Now the computer is in the hands of many talented individuals who can, in their spare time, turn out imaginative software for an eager market.

Developing software for this market was difficult. Custom packages were developed for particularly specialized professionals such as accountants and doctors. This is special applications software, as mentioned in Chapter 2. But this new market consisted of diversified groups. A new approach to software was needed to solve the problems of all these different users.

In any business there is a need to communicate in writing, to file and retrieve information, and to process financial transactions. These functions became the basis for special types of software that handled these tasks, but in a way that allowed the user to define his unique requirements. This group is the generalized application software defined in Chapter 2. They include word processing, file management, and financial management systems.

Generalized software is a major step away from the previous dependence on custom programming. Programming takes a great deal of training, and it takes a long time to develop a custom program. Generalized software is a tool that a relatively inexperienced person can use to develop systems that can work in fairly unique environments. Each type of software—word processing, file management, and financial management—addresses business applications handled well by the computer. They will, in fact, solve most of your data-handling business situations.

Faster computers with larger memories have now led to integrated systems. These are all-in-one systems that include the functions of word processing, file management, and financial analysis. The term *integration* is very confusing because it refers to many different ways of making systems work together. The purpose, however, is to provide you with a total business package in which each part can use the data and functions of the other parts.

You can expect to see some incredible developments in software in the next few years. The trend will be away from the technical and toward the easy-to-use, flexible software. Try to keep an open mind, following the software reviews in your favorite computer magazine.

3.2

WORD PROCESSING

Word processing is probably the most significant breakthrough in putting down words since man gave up chiseling stone and started writing on papyrus. The term *word processing* may sound somewhat ominous, but it is only a way of handling textual material in an efficient manner. Computers can change, move around, store, and retrieve characters, words, sentences, and even whole paragraphs very quickly. Using a word processor is similar to using a typewriter, but instead of putting the words on paper where they may have to be changed and the page retyped, words are typed into the computer's memory where they can be changed and rearranged at will. When displayed on a screen monitor, the words look much like a printed page. They are saved and stored on a disk, to be retrieved again for more changes or for printing on the printer. You'll never have to retype anything again.

A word processor also gives you a psychological advantage over the typewriter. You will find yourself typing faster, knowing that it is easy to correct mistakes. There is no bell and carriage return to interrupt your thoughts or pace; the word processor takes care of the margins and carriage returns. You will not be inhibited by the "blank" page because your text is not being permanently written and you can try different sentences or words.

The process of typing on the word processor is also faster because you do not necessarily have to be concerned with the format of the text. Your printer is instructed on how to print the text by format commands from the word processor. And these can be changed very easily. If you print something single-spaced and then decide you need it double-spaced with wider margins, you merely tell your word processor. It sets your printer to work printing the new version much faster than any human being can type. Go back, rearrange the text in the computer's memory, then put your printer to work printing out a clean, new copy.

All businesses must deal with typed words; the word processors make it easier. Text can be used over and over again. It can be modified for another purpose without going through the bother of retyping it. The computer can even be directed to merge the text with other files. Addresses in one computer file can be inserted into a standard letter body in another computer file. And always, the tireless printer continues turning out fresh individual copies.

Most word processors let you search for a specific word at electronic speeds. You could put a list of all your clients or pictures on a word processing file in the same way you would list them on sheets of paper. Your word processor could then search that file for any name or description you request. You can also use this search feature to make changes throughout your text. Let's say you have finished a long article and decide that you want to change every word "photograph" to the word "picture." Just give the proper instructions to your computer; within seconds, the word "picture" will replace the word "photograph" wherever it appears in the text.

Because of the flexible way computers and printers can represent and form characters, some systems can easily handle foreign-language character sets. You may want to take this into consideration if you do business in other countries. Even if your correspondence is conducted closer to home, you can often dress up your copy with boldface type or even italics. Your bills might have more impact, for example, if the amount due is printed in big, boldface type.

A word processing system alone makes writing a lot easier, but the extras that can be used with such a system can make even someone who flunked grade-school English into a halfway competent writer. These systems check and correct spelling, punctuation, and grammar, and will even suggest substitutes for overworked words.

3.3

FILE MANAGEMENT SYSTEMS

There are many types of file management systems, called by many different names. In brief, this category of software allows you to define the data you need in the format you want for your particular application, store it in your computer system, retrieve it by your designated criteria, change it, manipulate it, and print it selectively. All these may be performed by a single system or a series of systems. They may be called data base systems, filing systems, or indexing systems. Their function is to allow you to handle your data in your own way without resorting to customized programming.

These systems will handle any of the filing requirements you have, whether your files are on index cards or in manila folders in a filing cabinet. As with word processing systems, data are stored electronically so they can be easily changed. Whereas you are probably limited to a single filing order in your present method, file management systems often allow you to locate files in any order. You can easily set up your system to locate a client by a name or a number. It can also locate files on the basis of certain criteria, such as your New York state clients.

There are some file management functions that may come as part of a file management system or may be separate. The most useful of these is the *mail generation function*. This is where your word processing form letter collaborates with your file management file to generate personalized letters. It can address the envelopes for those letters or print up mailing labels for mass mailings. Most systems allow you to design your own output formats if you are using special preprinted forms or specially sized mailing labels.

The *report generation function* is another handy feature. You can selectively print detailed or summary information from your file. For example, you may want a list of everyone with outstanding bills, in order of date due, or of all the pictures you have of national parks. In fact, a report generator may open up all sorts of new information to you. In your present system, you would have to go through each one of your files, copy out information, put it into some sort of order, and maybe add up some numbers. The report generator can do this all for you in a matter of minutes; your printer, of course, prints it all out neatly.

3.4

FINANCIAL MANAGEMENT SYSTEMS

Financial management systems are better known as spreadsheets (as mentioned in Chapter 2), but their capabilities are expanding beyond the limited use of a simple spreadsheet. A spreadsheet, simply an accounting worksheet, has columns across the top and rows down the side; you write in your numbers where they intersect. You may already be using these worksheets to do your bookkeeping. That's exactly what a spreadsheet is, only bigger. Typically, it has 256 rows and sixty-four columns, although the dimensions vary quite a bit among software products. You lay it out and put in data just as you would with the old-fashioned paper type. But instead of doing the arithmetic yourself, the software does it for you. Big deal, you say? Well, it's the "what if" capability that excites everybody.

Let's say that you have used a spreadsheet to work up your business budget for the year. Naturally, you can't predict everything accurately, but you set up your model based on your best judgment. Now what if you make a terrific sale or incur an unexpected expense? Merely plug the new numbers into their appropriate boxes, and the system recalculates your entire budget based on these new figures. Now you can sit down and daydream of big sales and new equipment, seeing how it will affect your profits, courtesy of your spreadsheet model.

You can use your electronic spreadsheet in any way you might use a paper one. Just as with the word processing and file management systems, the main advantage is that it can easily be changed. The calculations are redone when any change is made, and, of course, you can get a printed copy any time you want one.

3.5

SPECIAL APPLICATIONS SOFTWARE

Special applications software is different from generalized software because it is specifically designed to perform a particular business job. Everything has been predetermined for you: the type of input you will put into the system, the data that will be kept in the files, the reports that will be printed, and the functions that will be performed. Special applications software is often referred to as *canned* software.

Though you can find some canned software for photography, it may not suit your business operations. But photography is a business like any other, and there exists applications software that will take care of pure business functions, especially in the area of accounting. Systems you can consider for your business are general ledger, accounts payable, accounts receivable, tax preparation, and, if you are running a large studio with a lot of equipment, an inventory system.

The nice part about special applications software is that it comes ready-made and is fairly easy to learn. As you do your research, keep an eye out for specialized software; you might find something that works perfectly for a particular function you want.

3.6

CUSTOM PROGRAMMING

If you find you have a task that is so unique that it can't be managed by your software, you can always resort to custom programming. For instance, you may not like any of the accounting software available and would like to set up your own system of bookkeeping on your computer. A special program would have to be written specifically to perform that task. Having it programmed will be expensive but may be the only alternative if you must have the task computerized. If you need to find a programmer, follow the suggestions in the section "Getting Professional Help" in Chapter 7.

What about doing some of your own custom programming? There are hundreds of books promising to turn you into a programmer overnight. Unless you really want to learn how to program, think you have the talent for it, and do have a great deal of time to put into it, don't bother. Skilled programmers earn a great deal of money doing what they do, and it took them many years to acquire that skill. Learning a few programming statements does not make you a programmer. You have to think logically, like a machine; you must learn how to approach certain problems and know the techniques for solving them. You must be able to get yourself out of trouble when things don't work out the way they should. This requires some understanding of the way the computer and the operating system work, as well as the limitations of the programming language.

Still, there may be some simple applications you might want to try yourself. If you have an application that is fairly simple and can't be handled by any of the available software, and if you have a lot of time and think you might enjoy it, then by all means go ahead and try some programming. Just avoid committing yourself to an important project only to discover you can't finish it.

4

GETTING DOWN TO BUSINESS

Now that you have some idea of what a computer can do, let's see how it can help you with your specific photography-business problems. The objective of this chapter is to identify some areas that lend themselves to automation, to help you organize your preparation for computerization, and to start you thinking about how to implement your business on a computer. Many of the suggestions are only examples of what you could do. Your business is similar to other businesses, but it is also unique in the way you do things. The actual techniques of developing your own computer systems will be covered in Chapter 8, Planning and Designing Your System.

4.1

GENERAL BUSINESS

No matter what type of photographer you are, you have to handle the sort of everyday clerical work common to any business. Don't hesitate to read how other businesses handle similar problems. It doesn't make any difference if the product is bird seed or photographs—many of the problems and the solutions are the same.

As you look at your business tasks, try to identify those that are *repetitive.* Look for items you often include when you are dealing with clients, such as your price list. Look through your file cabinet and review the types of information you store there. How often do you refer to those files? How often do you change them, and how difficult is it for you to make changes? Could you benefit from a summary of your files? This is how you need to start viewing your business. Now let's look at some specifics.

4.1.1 Correspondence

Nothing can strangle a business faster than paperwork. First of all, look at your volume of correspondence. A word processing system is vastly superior to a typewriter if you do any significant amount of letter writing, especially repetitive letter writing. If the letters are of the same type, you can use a word processing system to store the bodies of these letters in separate files and then simply include them in your new letter without having to retype them. If your letters go regularly to the same people, you could benefit from a word processor that interfaces with a file management and mail generating system. In this case, you write the body of the letter with your word processor; the mail generating system inserts the appropriate addresses from your file management system and addresses the envelopes. This last function is a dramatic time-saver if you send out numerous query letters, copies of your stock list, or promotional brochures.

The key to these systems is the mail generating and file management systems, but with a little ingenuity, a stand-alone word processing system will function quite well. If the word processing system supports multiple files and has a search capability, one file can actually be an address book. You simply search the address book for the name and address you want and then transfer it to the body of your letter and the appropriate location on the envelope. If you send out any promotional material, mail generators can be a real help. They can print out mailing labels of your total file or of selected groups on the basis of certain file information (such as all San Francisco clients or only calendar companies).

You probably have some standard forms that change infrequently. You either send them out as they are, or you modify them somewhat. These may be price lists, standard agreements, packing slips for transferring your photos, model releases, or invoices. You probably photocopy them now or, if your volume is high enough, have them printed. This may be the best way to handle these forms except if you do occasionally have to change them or add information to them. If you do, then a computer can make it easier.

You probably include with your photo submissions some sort of agreement schedule or a document which spells out the terms of your service. A stock photographer would want to include the rights that are being granted, the holding fees, damage fees, credit line requirements, and other items in the terms of submission. An assignment photographer might want to put together a statement spelling out his basic fees, expenses, advances and payments, how the photos are to be used (this can be changed for each client), return of outtakes, credit line, cancellations and postponements, reshoot fees, and anything else that may seem necessary to specify the terms of his assignment.

Is all this paper really necessary? Not always. Sometimes you can use your computer to send *electronic mail*. With electronic mail, you prepare your correspondence on your computer as if you were going to print and mail it; instead, you transfer it at electronic speeds over the telephone lines to another computer. The recipient can read it on his screen monitor or print it. Some networks will even accept correspondence and complete the delivery if your recipient doesn't have a computer. Electronic mail will be covered in more detail in Chapter 10, The Photo Networks. If your correspondent can be reached electronically and you need speedy communication, put electronic mail on your list.

4.1.2 Filing

No matter what type of photographer you are, you probably have some sort of client file. If you are a writer/photographer, your client file probably consists of publishers; if you are a stock photographer, you'll have a file of photo editors; even if you do work for hire, you probably maintain some sort of file on the clients for whom you are presently doing work, and maybe some you hope to serve in the future.

If you have your prospective clients' names on index cards, then you have some idea of the type of information you may need for such a system. In addition to the name and address of each client, you probably have written on the card what you have sent him and when, what his response was, and maybe what his picture interests are. Think about what other information might be useful to you and how you might simplify that information. Even before you purchase a computer, start recording onto the cards all the data which you might want, so that you won't have to go back later to find them. If you are just starting out, go to the library and look through some of the directories aimed at your markets, such as *Photographer's Market*, *Writer's Market*, *Literary Market Place*, *Magazine Industry Market Place*, and the *Gift and Decorative Accessory Buyers Directory*. If you see some value in sending your stock list or promotional material to a large number of people listed in those directories, then consider using a computer.

Don't overlook other files that you may want to maintain on a computer. These can include information resources, magazine and newsletter subscriptions, other photographers, equipment sources, model releases, and so on. Look through your present files. The files you are already maintaining should suggest some areas that would benefit from automation.

4.1.3 Billing and Collection

All photographers are concerned with client billing. If you use a standard invoice form, the only items that change are the names and addresses and the amounts due. You can put your standard form on a computer file, make the changes using your word processor, run it against your client file for the name and address, and print it out through your mail generator onto your letterhead.

If everybody paid his bills on time, you could stop there. However, there are always delinquent cases that need to be followed up. If you include a due date on your client file, it is an easy matter to have your computer select past-due bills from your client file. This can eliminate special reminder lists or the need to review all your clients for past-due items. This is especially handy if you are fortunate enough to have a lot of people owing you money. You can even carry the process one step further by having your computer select those past-due cases and automatically print the reminder notice to the client.

If you do not want to use generalized data management software, there are specialized billing systems and collection systems designed for small businesses. Research these carefully before you decide to purchase one. A billing and collection system programmed for a manufacturing operation may not work too well in your photographic business, especially if the system isn't very flexible. A system designed for a service industry, such as a lawyer's office, might work very well, especially if it was designed with enough flexibility to allow you to customize some of the terminology used in the printing process. You will have to comply with the rules built into the system and must maintain a separate billing file for the clients who owe you money. But as those systems are already set up to run billings, you do not have to do any work. They will automatically do any follow-up on delinquent clients, produce nice summary reports on your billing activity, and may even interface directly with an accounting system. If you do a large volume of billing, check into these specialized systems. You might find one perfect for your business.

4.1.4 Bookkeeping and Taxes

There is probably no task more disliked by photographers than the job of bookkeeping. You may even put it off until the end of the year and then face the monumental task of trying to figure out what each receipt was for. But accurate bookkeeping is an important part of doing business and very much to your advantage at tax time. Your typical expenses will be equipment (and its depreciation), film and developing, office supplies, postage, studio rental, education, travel expenses, and so on. On the other side, there is income: photo-use fees, royalties, advances, billed expenses, sales tax, and so on. For these tasks you can either have a custom program written, purchase an accounting package, or use a spreadsheet. Since a computerized system takes much drudgery out of bookkeeping and handles all the arithmetic for you, with one you are more likely to keep your bookkeeping current.

Whatever system you choose to use, make sure it will get you to the most important task: the preparation of your year-end taxes. When it comes to the actual preparation of your taxes, you can either use your spreadsheet or purchase a special tax preparation package. Because tax preparation is so standardized, your spreadsheet software may come with the tax forms already set up for you. You merely plug in the numbers; your computer handles the arithmetic.

There is nothing more standard than accounting, so shop around and look at the special application packages. Search for simple systems. You aren't a multicompany corporation, and you do not want to bother with the extra work of double-entry bookkeeping. Stick with the simple systems, which require only that you keep a record of your income and expenses. Look for packages specifically designed for small businesses or even for the home. They may suit your purpose very well.

4.1.5 Equipment Inventory

Whether you run a big studio or are a weekend photographer, you will want to set up an inventory system for all your equipment. You need it for insurance purposes and to record the depreciation for your taxes. A computer makes it easy for you to add new equipment and take out old equipment that you might sell.

If you have a lot of equipment, you might want to look at special applications software. Most, though, are designed for manufacturing firms or businesses with frequent stock changes. So unless you intend to keep track of every mailer and battery you own, or if you buy a new camera every week, these systems may be a little too much for your business. Actually, any one of the generalized software packages will do the job. You can simply list your equipment and its cost by using your word processor. Additions and changes can easily be made.

Or you might want to use your file management system. With it, you might set up one record called "cameras" that would show information for each of your cameras. You can also use your spreadsheet. List the equipment down the left side of the spreadsheet, dedicate one column to cost, put in your depreciation formulas, and let the software do the arithmetic.

4.1.6 Financial Planning

If you really want to stay on top of the profitability of your business, consider using your spreadsheet or a special application system for budgeting or cash flow analysis. You can put in values for your expected income and expenses, then project your economic situation into the future. You may be sure of some items, such as a sale of a picture to a magazine or calendar company that pays you on publication. For others, you may have to estimate based on what you expect to receive or spend in the future. These numbers can then be adjusted when you actually incur the income or expense, and the projection will automatically be adjusted. This helps you plan your future purchases of equipment when you know you will be in a better cash position. You will have a better idea of when you should increase your marketing efforts, and you can see the effects of the cost of a marketing program on the income you might realize from that effort. You can also use it as a tool to price your pictures or your services. If it turns out that your expenses are lower than you expected, you can reduce your fees to be more competitive; if your expenses turn out to be higher than you expected, you will want to increase your fees.

4.2 THE STOCK PHOTOGRAPHER

The information in this section is directed to the problems of the stock photographer, who shoots on speculation and then tries to sell photos from his files. If you are not a stock photographer, there still will be some things in this section that you might find valuable or that might suggest some solution to a unique problem of yours. Even if you primarily sell on assignment, you will also have your own personal pictures and outtakes that must be filed and that you will someday probably want to sell.

4.2.1 Your Photo Files

In what shape are your photo files? This is a good time to go through them all, throw out what you really can't use, and file the rest. If you don't have some sort of classification system, now's the time to start one. There are probably as many systems for cataloging photos as there are photographers, but no one has yet devised an ideal one. This is probably because the filing requirements vary with the type of subject matter. Ideally, it would be nice to come up with one system that works for all your photos. If you are a specialist, you can do this. An animal photographer needs to identify his photos by each animal's common name and scientific name. A travel photographer is more interested in classifying his or her pictures by country, city, and point of interest. But if you do both, you have a conflict. Actually, your best solution is to keep them in separate files with their own classification systems. It is also feasible to set them up on your computer this way. Your computer system need not follow your manual filing system. When I want to look up my animals in my computer system, I want to do it by common name, such as "koala." But my files are set up on the basis of their animal classification, so my koalas are manually filed under "marsupials." There are no conflicts as long as my computer file tells me where they are filed so I can find them. The same can be done for the computer travel file. If, under "Australia," I want to cross-reference "koalas," I can indicate that they are manually filed under "marsupials" in the animal file.

There are two approaches you can take to recording the photos themselves in your computer file: individually or as groups. Naturally, coding them individually is going to take a lot more work, but it will help you locate a specific photo more quickly. This would be the best approach if you work on assignment. If you are a heavy-volume stock photographer, you may wish to record some classifications of photos by groups. For instance, you may have a classification called "leisure activities"; under that you might have "hot-air balloons." After a recent trip to Albuquerque, you came back with five hundred pictures of balloons. Itemizing each one would be quite a task and unnecessary. Your computer system can have the category "hot-air balloons," which can be updated. If you want to, you can further subdivide it by location. Let's say that several of these photos become hot sellers and you want to keep records on them individually. For this purpose, you could set up a subsidiary file that would allow you to keep statistics on individual special photos.

Having separate files for different classifications of photos is not a problem unless you want to bring them together for a consolidated stock list. Your file management system may be able to pull data from different filing systems, then print that information on a single report. If not, you may need some custom programming done.

If you shoot in black and white, you'll need to cross-reference your prints to your negatives. It makes no difference in what manual order you decide to file your negatives as long as there is a numbering scheme that identifies their physical locations of all negatives on that subject. You can also design your picture file to include printing data. That way, if you need to print more copies, all the printing information will be instantly available to you.

Model releases can also be a problem. If you need these, set up a manual way of filing the releases with some sort of identification number. Include that number in your computer picture file system so you'll know if a picture has a release and is readily available.

4.2.2 Stock Lists

As a stock photographer, you'll want to generate a stock list from your computer file. As you think about how to organize and classify your photos, also think about how you want this information to look on your stock list. You may want to list your animals alphabetically by common name. Your travel photos might be listed by country, then by city under country. If you have a different clientele for each category, you may want more than one stock list, each directed toward the interests of particular clients. On the other hand, you might need a composite list and have to consider how you will merge the two, or how you might do it manually.

If you don't want to or can't generate a stock list directly for your computer picture file, then you can use your word processing system. For something like this, it is again far superior to the typewriter. You will still have to type every classification in the order you want, but you can move everything around very easily to different columns or positions. Plus, once you have your stock list on your word processing system, you can easily revise it.

4.2.3 Captioning Photos

A computer can help you with the tedious task of captioning your photographs. If the captions are unique to each photo, it will only help you as much as a typewriter would. If, however, there is some repetition, it can be a real time-saver. If you are a wedding, portrait, or assignment photographer, you might want to include your client's name and address and maybe a job number on each photo. A computer can easily use your client file to pick up this information, printing it on labels as often as you require. The printing process can also be interrupted so that you enter, on the keyboard, information unique to a picture. If you need to caption slides, you will need a matrix printer that prints in a very small, compressed mode of seventeen characters to the inch so that the information will fit on a half-inch label. This can be done by writing a very simple, custom program. It is a real time-saver if you have to make up labels for those five hundred hot-air balloons!

4.2.4 Follow-up

A stock photographer deals with hundreds of photos sent out to dozens of clients. He has to keep track of who has been sent what and when, which photos have been returned and which are being held, and which photos are going to be used and how; plus he must be able to follow up on all of this. The problem is manageable if you do a small amount of business but can get out of hand if you have many clients.

You probably use some sort of system now, maybe index cards. These cards can be the source for your computer conversion, but right now think about the information you have on those cards and what other information might be useful that you haven't covered. Make sure you have included dates for follow-up activity. The computer can keep track of what was sent and will remind you when you have to follow up. If you want to become sophisticated and the volume of your business warrants it, the computer can also automatically produce the follow-up correspondence. As photos are returned to you, you can easily delete them, leaving the ones the client is retaining.

4.2.5 Locating Picture Needs

The purpose of most of your correspondence is to find out what pictures clients need. Often, a client needs a picture very quickly and will contact either an agent or a photographer who is known to him. As a freelance stock photographer, you may lose out on many picture sales just because you were not aware of what clients needed. Now there is a more timely way clients can communicate their picture needs—by posting their latest *want lists* on a network. Networks offering this service are covered in Chapter 10, The Photo Networks. Even with an inexpensive computer, you can query these services via any telephone and have the appropriate pictures in the mail the same day. If you do not have the pictures in your file, you may have time or be in the necessary location to take the pictures the client needs.

4.2.6 Stock Agents

Stock agents are also using this facility. Agents get hundreds of requests for pictures they do not have in their files. They put their lists on these networks; you might just have the picture they are looking for. In the future, agents will keep fewer pictures in stock because the networks will enable them to locate pictures quickly. If you work through an agent, this will allow you to retain more of your photos for your own marketing efforts while still getting the benefits of the agent's marketing contacts.

If you do have a stock agent, you probably send him hundreds of photos on a regular basis, and you likely inventory them with numbers for record-keeping purposes. Your agent keeps some and returns the rest. At some time, your agent may give you the numbers he or she assigned to your pictures. If your original list to the agent came from your computer, it is an easy matter to mark the ones the agent retained and to include the number the agent assigned to those photos. If you are also selling your own pictures, you may have similars or duplicates of the pictures your agent has on file. If either you or your agent negotiates an exclusive agreement on a photo, this record will be the way you and your agent can identify the photo. If, at the end of your contract with the agent, you wish to terminate the contract and have your photos returned to you, your number record would be an easy pull-sheet for your agent. You would get your photos back much faster.

4.3

ASSIGNMENT PHOTOGRAPHERS

An assignment photographer is anyone who takes pictures specifically requested by a client and is paid for doing that service. This can include wedding photographers, portrait photographers, freelance photojournalists, magazine photographers, advertising photographers, or anyone who works on a for-hire basis.

4.3.1 Pricing a Job

Pricing your jobs can be tricky. If you've been in business awhile, your fees are probably pretty well set. But if you are just starting out, it may be quite difficult to come up with realistic fees; some photographers end up pricing themselves too low to make a profit. Spreadsheet software is tailor-made for this problem. Some already incorporate a professional fee-analysis schedule. You will want to modify it to suit your individual needs, but it will suggest some things you may overlook—and all the formulas are already built into it. Essentially, you list all expected overhead expenses for the year (rent, phone, postage, equipment, and so on); expenses directly attributable to a photo job, such as film and developing;

the number of jobs you expect to get in a year; and what income you expect to realize. Once that is plugged into the spreadsheet analysis, you should have a fair idea of what you will have to charge per job to make your expected profit. The nice thing about a spreadsheet is that you can change the parameters for "what if" circumstances to see what the results might be.

As you gain experience in costing out a job, you can easily change the numbers in your spreadsheet to come up with more realistic fees. For example, you may need a separate cost analysis for each type of job you do. If you are a wedding photographer, you have the extra cost of frames, albums, and special printing that you incur with each job. If you shoot for the local chamber of commerce, your costs might consist only of film, developing, and travel expenses. If you are a portrait photographer, you have the expense of setting up a studio, which will be allocated to many clients over a period of time.

It is also a good idea to keep spreadsheet cost data on the *actual* income and expense of each job. That way you can analyze your profit experience. Some jobs will be more profitable than others; with a spreadsheet you can identify the reasons why. There also may be great uncontrollable variances in the profitability of each job, but at least you can determine an average on which to base your pricing structure.

4.3.2 Scheduling

As an assignment, wedding, or portrait photographer, you will want to keep track of your appointments. The computer can set up your appointments and keep your schedule up-to-date. At the beginning of each day you can get a list of what you have to do for the day, week, or month.

Scheduling can be set up by your word processor or a special scheduling system. Since many of the small portable computers come with a scheduler built in, you can take the computer with its built-in schedule with you from job to job. The convenience of a computer schedule is the ease of changing it. If you constantly modify your schedule to the point that it is barely legible, consider the advantages of using a nice, neat computer schedule.

4.3.3 Finding Assignments

Some of the photo networks list clients who are looking for photographers to do assignment work. If you travel frequently, a small portable computer and any telephone will help you to check on the needs of those clients. It is cheaper for the client to hire a photographer this way because the photographer is already at the location where they need the picture. This saves them the considerable expense of sending a photographer to the location. If you list your services and location on these networks—which you can do from anywhere in the world—you can constantly keep prospective clients informed of your whereabouts.

Even if you do not stray too far from home, you can list your services on a local electronic bulletin board. Some local networks, especially set up to provide this service, are called *electronic Yellow Pages*. You can advertise in them just as you would the regular Yellow Pages. People access them by using their own computers. As more people start using computers, this service will become more valuable.

4.4

WRITER/PHOTOGRAPHER

If you are a writer/photographer, a word processing system is well worth the investment. You will write faster and better. Making corrections and changes, and moving text from one section to another, are done so easily that you will wonder how you ever wrote without a computer. Some publishers now indicate a preference for receiving manuscripts on diskettes. They can put them on their own computer and, using their own word processor, edit them faster. The savings in typesetting costs are tremendous. Since there is a microprocessor in the typesetting machine, it is easier to simply feed in the edited manuscript in machine-readable form, eliminating the need to transcribe the information and avoiding the subsequent errors. The section on word processing in Chapter 6, Evaluating Software, will give you some idea of the power and versatility of these systems.

4.4.1 Computer-Assisted Writing

A word processing system will not only help you with the mechanics of getting words on paper, but also change the way you write. Never again will you have to face a blank page in a typewriter. If you're not sure how to start, just jump in and write. You can always stick the beginning in later—without retyping anything. What if you have several lead-in sentences you want to use but you can't choose one? Put them all down and later select the one you like best. The others are easily deleted. No need to interrupt the flow of your creativity. If you reach a snag or an area where you have to do more research, just mark it in the text and come back to it later. Your main concern is to get your words and ideas down. It is simple to insert material or rearrange things later; the joy of it is that you don't have to retype anything. You may even become a better writer, because you can endlessly edit and improve your text.

One problem, though, is that because you can rearrange everything later, you may have a tendency not to plan your text before you sit down at the keyboard. But now there is software to help you with that problem, too. This software leads you through an outlining procedure, developing an outline template that is displayed on your screen. You simply follow the outline as you write so that you don't stray from your plan. The template does not become part of your text. Even without the outline software, you can develop an on-screen outline and just delete the outline when you are finished.

If you write articles, you probably rework them to sell to different markets. Let's say you have written an article for a major national publication. It's on a hot topic, and you could realize more income by writing an article on the same subject for your local newspaper. No need to do all that retyping—just bring the original article back up on your word processor and rework it.

The computer takes a lot of the drudgery out of writing. It is not necessary to interrupt your writing to look up the spelling of a word in the dictionary. Your *spelling checker* program will scan your text later and pick out any misspelled words or typing errors. Some will even look up the spelling for you and make the correction in your text.

There are also *grammar checkers* that will review grammatical points such as tense agreements, punctuation, or duplicate words. Your grammar checker may also have a *style checker* that can flag overly long sentences or clichéd phrases. It can also measure the reading level of your writing by applying formulas of average word size and sentence length to your text.

If you are writing a book, your word processor may have an *index facility* that allows you to tag words you want indexed. It will alphabetize those words and give you the page references. Some indexers will go through your entire text, select common English words, alphabetize them, tell you how frequently they are used, and give their page locations. The edited list then becomes an index.

4.4.2 Research

You probably do most of your research at your local library. But wouldn't it be convenient to do all the research from your own home, especially when you are in the middle of writing something and realize you have to verify a particular fact? Many of the networks publish electronic encyclopedias, newspapers, newsletters, and all sorts of information that is as near as your computer. You merely dial the network on your telephone, and there it is on your screen. If the material is lengthy, print it out on the printer.

4.5

KEEPING TECHNICAL DATA

Your computer can also be used to keep track of the technical data needed in actual photographic work. A small portable computer is ideal for this; it's easily taken to the actual work location. If you have both a small portable and a large business computer and want to save this information on the larger system, it is not difficult to cable the computers together to transfer the information.

4.5.1 In the Darkroom

The darkroom is an excellent place to use your computer for recordkeeping. As you print pictures, you will want to make notes on type of paper, type of developer, exposure time, procedures such as dodging or burning in, and modifications of normal developing procedures. If you are printing in color, you will also want to note which color correction packs you used. If you use some of your own chemical formulas, you'll want to keep that information handy while you are working.

Your computer can keep an inventory of supplies used, such as paper and chemicals. (You don't want to run out of No. 3 paper in the middle of a job.) As you use your supplies, enter that information into the computer. When it comes time to do more darkroom work, the computer inventory will warn you when you are running short on items.

4.5.2 In the Field

A portable computer can keep track of technical data while you're in the field. Many of the portables are small enough to be hand carried and are run on batteries so you can take them anywhere. You might want to note the exposure information for some of your photographs, especially if you do very technical work. You can use it for captioning to note information on subject matter or location. If you are a photographer/writer, you might want to keep notes to use to write articles.

You can load tables of technical data into your computer for reference in the field. These can include nighttime exposure, depth of field, bellows factors, reciprocity failure adjustments, filter factors, Kelvin color correction, or any other technical data that you may need to refer to in your type of photography.

You now have some ideas about how you might use a computer in your photographic business. The next two chapters will cover the actual selection of your computer hardware and, in more detail, the features of the various types of software products. As you make your hardware and software decisions, keep in mind how you will actually use them in your business.

5

SELECTING A COMPUTER

When you bought your camera, you based your selection on its features and what compatible accessories were available. All cameras take pictures. When it comes to computers, all of them move data around. Your computer choice will be based on all the components of the system, including software and peripheral hardware.

People often choose computers for many of the same reasons they choose cameras. If they buy a camera or a computer because of its name, they are buying a status symbol and are willing to pay extra money for a name and capabilities they may never need. This isn't the worst reason for buying something. Because a status name attracts buyers, secondary vendors are quick to capitalize on the situation and develop products for it, so you automatically get more choices.

Photographers are also notorious gadget lovers. Many just want the latest-model camera with everything that technology can put on it and, again, are willing to pay for the novelty. It may be important to them that their camera have a built-in digital clock and calculator and says, "Watch the birdie," or, "You are out of film." The same is true of people who buy computers.

A more intelligent approach is to evaluate your personal needs to choose the computer system that fits them. You will want to consider your present needs, your future needs (so that you will not grow out of your system too soon), and what you really can afford. You only need a computer that does the job you want done; anything more, and you could be wasting money.

As you think about buying a computer, you probably are considering some other things you might want to do with a personal computer.

You may have a teenager who would like to play games, or a young child who could benefit from educational software. So you try to consider these things as well as your business needs in your decision. *Don't.* Get the kids their own computer (or a home computer for yourself if you like to play the games). Your computer is a *business* computer. You don't want to have to compete with the rest of the family to use it. Also, since it is a business investment, you are going to want to make full use of its tax advantage as a depreciable asset and as an investment tax credit. Besides, computers designed for home use don't have the same capabilities as those designed for business use; most business computers just don't have that much game or educational software written for them. The exception to this would be if you are a weekend photographer who only occasionally uses the computer for business, or if you only want a computer to check into an on-line network.

5.1

TYPES OF COMPUTERS

There are three types of computers. Large *mainframe* computers are the ones that turn out all those bills you receive each month or answer the phone when you dial into a network. Mainframe computers are expensive and require a special environment plus a whole team of human professionals to service them.

Minicomputers are used in smaller businesses where several users may need to use the system at the same time. They are less expensive than the mainframes, do not require a special environment, and can be maintained by an experienced user with only the occasional services of a professional.

The *microcomputer* is the machine that started the revolution that has now brought the computer into homes and small businesses that could not begin to justify the cost of a larger computer. They are relatively inexpensive—and getting less expensive all the time—are reliable, require very little care, and can be totally maintained and used by a relatively inexperienced user. The microcomputer is the one for you.

The heart of the microcomputer is the microprocessor. There are actually only a handful of microprocessors on the market and they all perform very reliably. Of all the different makes and models of computers out on the market today, if you look under the hood, you will probably find the same microprocessors. Microprocessors vary in their internal operating speed and the amount of memory they can directly address. You will hear references to "8-bit," "16-bit," and "32-bit" machines. These terms apply to the internal way the microprocessor handles or transmits data. A 16-bit microprocessor with 8-bit data handling may be called a 16-bit or an 8-bit machine, while a 32-bit machine which transmits data 16 bits at a time may be called a 32-bit machine by some and a 16-bit machine by others.

Unfortunately, this confusing terminology cannot be avoided, because in choosing a computer you will want to consider the type of microprocessor running the system. A single 8-bit microprocessor can directly address 65,536 bytes (or characters) of memory, so essentially it is limited to 64K memory, though many 8-bit computers use extra processors so they can access more memory. The memory size limits the software that can be used by a particular machine. The software requirements can exceed the memory capacity of some machines, though that can sometimes be circumvented by "swapping" portions of the software in and out of memory. The 16-bit processors are faster and can have a great deal more memory. Potentially, they can be four times as fast as their 8-bit counterparts.

First, let's look at speed. If you are typing on a computer keyboard or on-line to a network, your computer isn't really doing much no matter how slow it is. It is capable of doing millions of operations while you are just trying to decide what key to depress on the keyboard. Even when it is not waiting for you to make up your mind, the computer can be slowed down by the speed capacity of the printer, the time it takes to access data from a disk, or the slow transmission rate over a telephone line. The only time you may notice some degradation is if you have a *process-bound* program, which does a lot of internal operations with little input/output activity. For the most part, a relatively slower processor will not bother you. You will be frustrated more by the slowness of data retrieval from the disk.

Memory capacity will be a more significant factor. As newer, more sophisticated, integrated software is developed, it will require memory capabilities beyond 64K. But a great deal of software has been developed for the 8-bit machines, and the 16-bit machines are just catching up. The 8-bit machine is usually less expensive, and since it has been around a long time, its software has been used and perfected.

Actually, many machines offer both 8-bit and 16-bit microprocessors (remember, this is the least expensive part of the system), so you can use all that tried and true 8-bit software as well as all that jazzy new 16-bit software. If you do make a choice one way or the other, it is not irrevocable. Private enterprise, being what it is, will provide a service if there is a demand. With a little software and hardware enhancement, your 8-bit machine can function with a 16-bit microprocessor and your 16-bit computer can be an 8-bit machine.

Though most of the computers you will be considering will come "packaged" with microprocessor and peripherals built in, we will cover each component separately so you will be in a better position to evaluate different configurations.

5.2

KEYBOARDS

Actually, you may have more difficult choices when it comes to the peripheral machinery, such as keyboards. Probably every computer has a different keyboard that some designer considered better than anyone else's keyboard. So first, let's narrow the field a little.

The keyboard is your basic medium of communication with the computer. There are two types of keyboards. One is a *membrane-type board* where pressure on a spot on the membrane causes a connection. Don't even consider this type. Because you can't feel the key depression, you have to watch the keyboard as you input data, and this will slow you down. The second type is a *contact* (or mechanical switch) keyboard, much like an electric typewriter. The less expensive "chicklet" type of contact keyboard does not give you enough feedback when you depress the keys and, like the membrane type, will slow you down. Even good feedback keyboards are going to feel different, so try them out. Some keyboards are stiffer than others, so if you are used to pounding on a manual typewriter, you may find letters constantly doubling up on you if the keyboard is too soft.

Look for a full "business" keyboard that has all the special characters. Check the special characters against the list of ASCII characters in Appendix A to make sure you are getting a complete character set. Be certain that the letters and the numbers are in the same place as they are on a regular typewriter keyboard. Make sure the keyboard is the same size as a typewriter and that the keys are not too close together. Even if you type with your thumbs, you will become very quick on a computer keyboard if it is properly designed. Also, check the lock-up keys, such as the one used for uppercase letters, for some sort of light so you'll know when they are locked up.

When working on a computer, you control your position on the screen monitor by moving a flashing dash or a box on the screen called a *cursor.* Your keyboard should have cursor control keys, usually represented by four arrows pointed in four different directions: up, down, right, left. If you will be putting in lots of numbers, look for a keyboard with a ten-key numeric pad like those found on electric calculators.

There are some keys you must have on a computer keyboard: the *escape* key (ESC), the *control* key (CTRL), and the *enter* or *return* key (ENT or RET). The control and enter keys are used constantly. The enter key should be located in the same area as the carriage return key on your typewriter, and should be large enough so you don't accidentally hit the surrounding keys. You will use this key to release data to the computer, or as a return key when using your word processor. The control key is usually on the opposite side, and it is frequently used in conjunction with other keys, such as letters.

Some computer keyboards are designed primarily for word processing and may have keys designated for word processing commands, like DELETE WORD or PAGE UP. Keyboards designed for more general use will have a group of function keys that are labeled F1, F2, F3, and so on. Their actual functions will be determined by the software in use at the time. If the software you want only uses function keys, then you better make sure your keyboard supports function keys; otherwise, function keys are a convenience but not a necessity. Chapter 6, Evaluating Software, will cover function keys in more detail.

If you bounce back and forth from your typewriter to your computer, you may prefer to have the special characters arranged the same way they are on your typewriter. There are, though, so many variations in special character locations that this may not be significant to you.

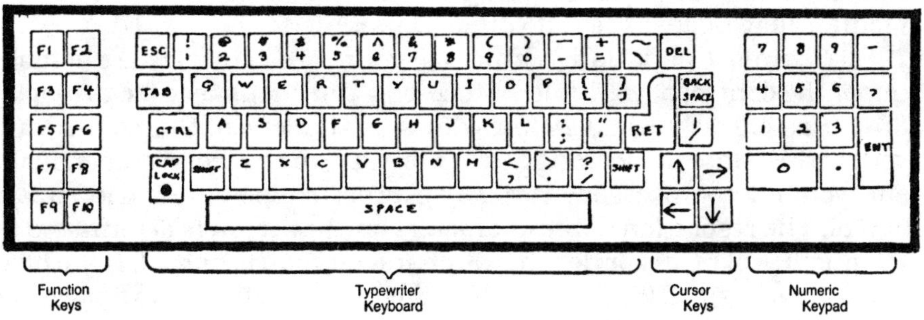

5-A. Typical Computer Keyboard

Many computers come with fixed keyboards; that is, the keyboard is physically joined to the computer housing. There are, however, some advantages to having a movable keyboard. In fixed systems, the keyboard may be too close to the screen for comfortable viewing. If the keyboard is movable, you can place it wherever you find it most comfortable. Personally, I put an eighteen-foot cord on mine, and when I'm taking notes while doing research, I do so from the comfort of my recliner.

Movable keyboards are usually connected to the computer by a standard handset telephone cord.

Keyboards are sold as part of the computer, so if your heart is set on a particular computer, you will probably have to accept the keyboard that comes with it. If your computer is a very popular one with a poor keyboard design, you may be able to purchase a better one from an independent manufacturer. Judging the keyboard is just one of the many factors you must consider when making your final computer choice.

5.3

SCREEN MONITORS

If you are thinking of buying a computer that uses your TV set as a screen monitor, forget it. The resolution of a TV screen is poor and will be totally unsuitable for anything you plan to do with a computer. Also, TV screens only display 40 characters across. If you are using a word processor, a printed line of text will probably be 60 to 65 characters across.

Screen monitors come in 4- or 5-inch sizes on portable computers, and in 9- or 12-inch sizes on full-size computers. The 9- or 12-inch sizes are better for prolonged usage, but try them for yourself. A 4-inch monitor may be just great if you are farsighted.

The most important features of your screen display are actually under the control of your microprocessor. You should be able to display 80 characters across and 24 lines down on the screen. Unless you want your correspondence looking as if it were done by a second grader, make sure your microprocessor lets you display both uppercase and lowercase letters. The resolution of the characters on the screen is determined by the number of *pixels* or dots in the character matrix or grid. If the pixel matrix is very small (5x7 pixels), the screen will not be able to display the descending portions of letters such as *y*, *p*, or *g*. This can make your text very difficult to read. The more pixels in the matrix (5x9 or more), the easier it will be to read the text. Compare similar characters such as *v* and *u* to see if you can distinguish the two easily.

What about the color? A high-resolution color monitor is very expensive, and you really have little use for it. A monochromatic monitor is a lot easier on your eyes for all the down-to-earth business work you will be doing. Monochromatic monitors come in black and white, green phosphorus, amber, and smoke. Black and white is the least desirable since over a period of time it can tire your eyes. Green is a popular choice, but amber has its devotees. How about reverse video, black on a green or amber background? Some software may depend on your monitor having this facility. It is useful for highlighting certain information; however, it is undesirable to have the whole screen in reverse video since you'll find it very hard on your eyes. Make sure there is some sort of control that allows you to adjust the contrast for your own comfort.

In totally self-contained systems, your monitor will be permanently fixed to a base. Sit down at the machine and make sure the height and distance are comfortable for reading. It will also be convenient if you can adjust the angle of the monitor.

5.4

MASS STORAGE

There are two problems with your computer memory: it has limited capacity, and when you turn off your computer, you lose all your data. This is impractical if you want to save anything after a session. To solve this problem, you must have some sort of mass storage device.

The cheapest is *tape*, quite similar to the tape in your cassette recorder. There are two problems with using this type of storage: it is very slow, and it must be accessed sequentially. In other words, if the information you need is at the end of the tape, then you have to read the entire tape to get to it. For your purposes, don't use a tape medium.

Your other choice is a *disk* or *diskette*. A disk is coated with a magnetic oxide that stores the bits of data by having the oxide particles polarized in one direction or another. The standard disk used on microcomputers is what is called a *floppy disk*.

There are several sizes of floppy disk. The 8-inch size, the 5¼-inch (sometimes referred to as a *minifloppy*), and the 3- or 3½-inch, less popular size sometimes used with portable computers (referred to as the *microfloppy*). The 8-inch disk holds the most data and has the advantage of having a standard IBM format. The 5¼-inch disks, less expensive and more commonly used on the newer-model computers, have no common format, although there should be some steps toward standardization as one or more computers start dominating the industry.

The problem with nonstandard formats is that a disk formatted for one computer cannot be read by another computer, even though they use the same type of disk. There are ways around this problem, though. There is software available that converts the format of one disk to that of another. A different way of circumventing this problem is to put the two computers in direct communication with each other, by a direct cable or via modems over communication lines. (See Chapter 10, The Photo Networks.) Data then transferred from one computer's memory to the other can be stored on the receiving computer's disk, using that disk's own format.

Think of a floppy disk as a 45-rpm record. In concentric circles around the disk, like the tracks of a record, are the tracks of the disk. The disk's pie-shape divisions are called *sectors.*"

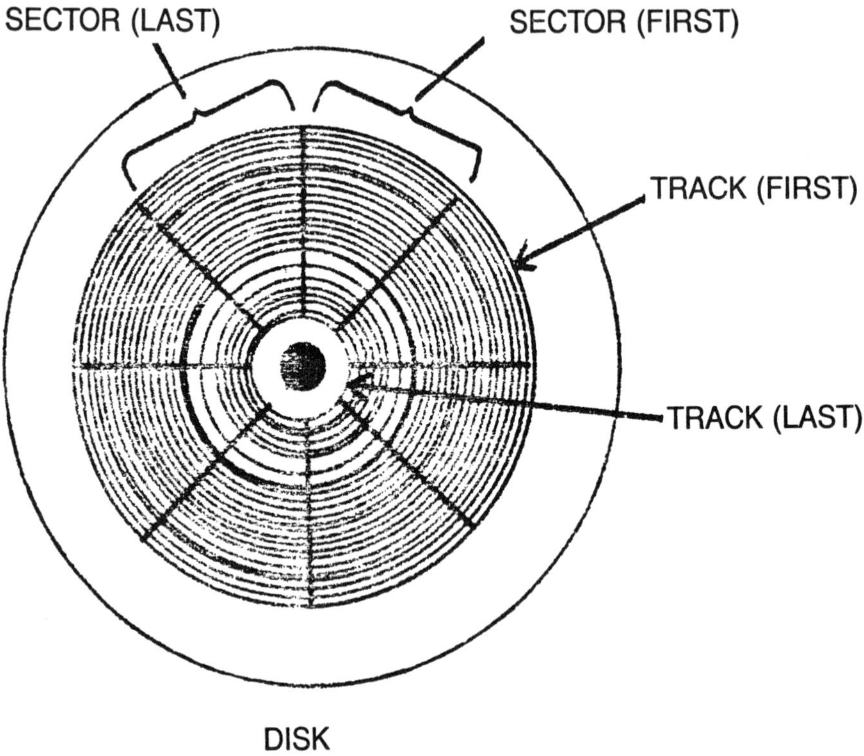

5-B. Disk Sectors and Tracks

The floppy disk is protected by a special stiff, permanent paper jacket. A special coating on the jacket's interior helps keep the disk free of dust. An access slot is cut in the jacket so the read/write heads of the disk drive can access the data. In addition, there are two alignment slots, a write-protect notch, and an index hole (or holes). When the write-protect notch is open on an 8-inch disk, data can be read or retrieved from the disk but not written or transferred to it. This protects valuable software and data from being inadvertently overwritten. It is just the opposite on the 5¼-inch disks. On these, when the notch is *covered*, the disk is protected.

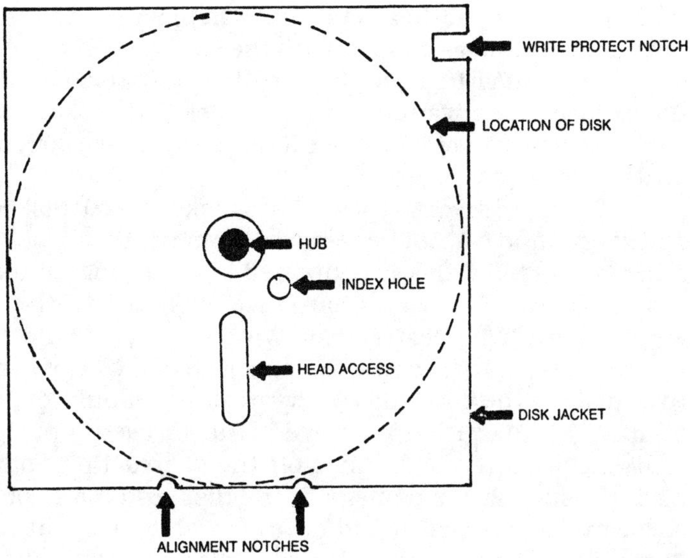

5-C. Disk in Jacket

Disks may be *hard sectored* or *soft sectored.* A soft-sectored disk has one index hole to indicate the starting position of the tracks. A hard-sectored disk has one index hole per sector. To make things even more interesting, disks can either be *single density* or *double density*—the double density, of course, being capable of holding more data. They can also be *single sided* or *double sided;* that is, data can be written on one or both sides of the disk. You may occasionally see the term *dual density.* This means that the disk drive can read and write to both single- and double-density disks. When you buy your diskettes, you may find a code on the box. SS/SD is single sided, single density; SS/DD is single sided, double density; DS/DD is double sided, double density.

DISKETTE CAPACITY

Disk Size	*Single Density*	*Double Density*
5¼" single sided	100-125K	150-250K
5¼" double sided	200-250K	300-500K
8" single sided	300-400K	700-800K
8" double sided	600-800K	1400-1600K

Note: The actual capacity depends on the way a particular computer system formats a disk.

More and more personal computers are using hard disks, sometimes referred to as "platters." With floppy disk drives, the read/write head actually makes contact with the surface of the disk. With the hard disks, the read/write head floats within a thousandth of an inch above the surface. The advantage of a hard disk is that it can hold much more data than a floppy, and because it revolves much faster, data access time is also a lot faster.

There are several types of hard disks. A fixed disk is contained in a sealed unit and cannot be removed from the disk read/write device. Another type of hard disk is contained in a cartridge and can be removed from the drive. The type of hard disk most used with personal computers is called a "Winchester" disk. Winchester is not the name of the manufacturer, but rather of the technology used. One of the problems with fixed disks is the hovering read/write head. Should it encounter a speck of dusk, a human hair, a fingerprint, or even a particle of cigarette smoke, the head may bounce off the obstruction and crash into the disk, causing severe damage to the disk and a loss of your data. Winchester disks are sealed and have special lightweight heads that press gently against a specially lubricated disk surface, virtually eliminating head crash problems. A Winchester disk can give you from five to over one hundred megabytes of storage capability. (A megabyte equals 1,048,576 bytes.)

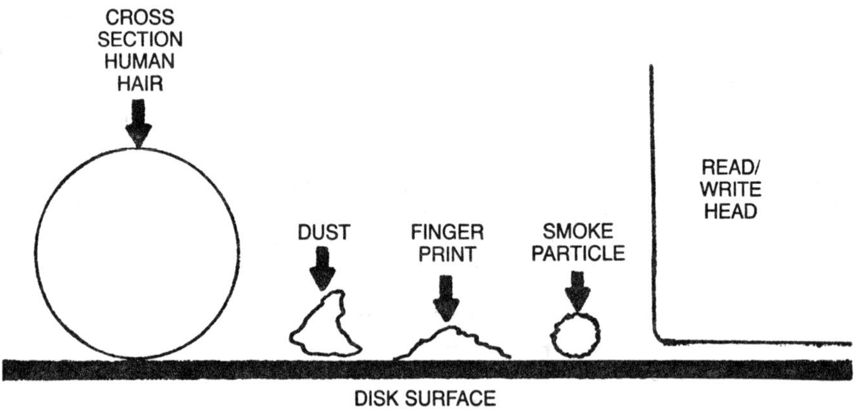

5-D. Foreign Material on Disk Surface

So which are better: floppy disks or fixed disks? Floppy disks are less expensive and convenient for organizing and filing your software and files. However, you do need a lot of them and you will find yourself constantly changing disks. Hard disks are faster when it comes to accessing data—anywhere from two to twenty times faster. They hold a great deal more data and software and are more convenient to use. They are, however, much more expensive, adding one thousand dollars or more to your computer cost. If you choose a floppy disk system, you can add a fixed disk system later.

5.5

PRINTERS

The components that we have discussed so far usually come packaged together in a single cabinet. The printer, however, is a separate component and will probably be the most expensive part of your system. There are several types of printers, but you should consider only two types: *letter quality* and *dot matrix.*

Letter-quality printers are exactly what the name implies. They produce high-quality printed output quite similar to that produced by your electric typewriter. There are two types of letter-quality printers. In one, the printing element is a *thimble* ,which spins until the desired letter is in place; then a small hammer makes an impact of that letter against the ribbon and paper. The second type is a *daisy wheel*, which has characters at the ends of its "petals." Letter-quality printers are very expensive and are quite slow. You are probably going to spend a thousand dollars or more for a printer that prints from fifteen cps (characters per second) to seventy cps. This, though, is quite a bit faster than you can type. Most people type eight to ten cps.

A dot matrix printer is much less expensive and a lot faster than a letter-quality printer. Prices start at a few hundred dollars, and the dot matrix printer can print from thirty to more than two hundred characters per second. The letters are formed in a dot matrix pattern similar to the way they are formed on your screen monitor. Some matrix printers produce poor-quality print because the dots do not blend together. For your own use this is fine, but if you are going to be sending correspondence or manuscripts out to clients, this will be unacceptable. The print is difficult to read, and some people resent getting documents that have obviously been prepared by a computer. However, the quality of these printers is improving, and it is possible to get a high-density matrix printer that looks quite good. Some printers improve the quality even more by moving a fraction after printing a character and then overprinting it to eliminate the spaces between the dots.

Because these printers form letters with a matrix pattern, there is no need to change the print element for different typefaces. Everything is managed by the printer's built-in microprocessor. Larger or smaller

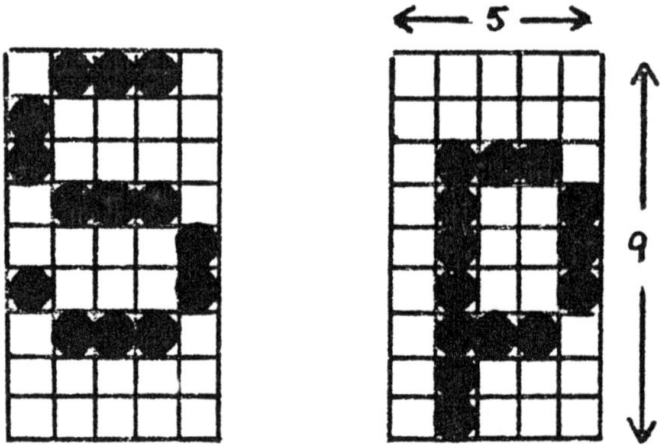

5-F. *Character Formation on a 5x9 Matrix*

characters, italics, and even foreign characters can be printed. Because they microspace by moving just a fraction of a distance, they can overtype and produce boldface type, super- and sub-script, and proportionally spaced letters across the page. Not all these options are available on all matrix printers, so if you need any of them, make sure the printer you are considering gives you these options.

Printers can handle paper of different widths. For your purposes you will need one that prints 80 characters across. If you are going to be doing a lot of report or spreadsheet printing, you might prefer a printer that can handle 132 characters across or more. Paper is passed through the printer in two ways. Single sheets of paper can be friction-fed to the printer in much the same way as you feed paper into your typewriter. You'll want this option, since you'll want to print your correspondence on your regular letterhead and be able to print on envelopes, postcards, labels, etc. If you are going to be printing a lot of material like a book, reports, lists, and so on, you will want to get a printer with a tractor feed. A tractor feed allows you to use continuous-form, perforated paper for the longer printing jobs. If you send out massive mailings on your letterhead, you might want to consider getting your letterhead printed on continuous-form paper.

5.6

CABLES AND INTERFACES

Most of your peripheral devices will come packaged together and all hooked up for you. There will, however, be some that you will have to connect to your computer. A computer connection is called an interface, and there are two methods of interfacing: *parallel* and *serial.*

With a serial interface, a character is transmitted one bit at a time. Your serial plug is a twenty-five-wire connection. Only two wires are actually necessary for the transmission, but the other wires are used to make sure the transmission was completed successfully and for other "handshaking" involved in establishing the connection (more on serial interfaces in Chapter 10, The Photo Networks). The industry standard is the *RS-232 interface.* Slower peripherals such as the screen monitor, modems for telephone communications, and the printer, are usually plugged into a serial interface because of the slow, bit-by-bit transmission. The serial interface is less likely to produce error into the transmission. The cable connection can be as long as two hundred feet—if you really can't stand to have your printer in the same room with you.

With a parallel interface, the entire 8-bit character is transmitted. This makes for faster transmission and so is used to interface with faster devices such as disk drives. Though speed is not a factor, many printers are also connected to parallel interfaces. Parallel interfaces, less expensive to set up, are found on less expensive printers. The parallel interface is a twelve-wire plug; the cable cannot be longer than twenty feet. Beyond that, there is too much "cross talk" interference.

Your computer should at least have one serial interface (of the RS-232 type) and one parallel interface. If you plan on purchasing a serial printer and using a modem, then you will want two serial plugs, because otherwise you'll have to unplug the printer when you are using the modem. If your computer does not have these interfaces or if you need more than is provided, you will need to purchase an *expansion interface board.* Your computer salesperson is the best person to talk to about what is needed for your particular computer.

5.7

PORTABLES

If you are a traveling photographer, you might want to consider the portable computer—handy for taking notes away from home or for hooking into your on-line photo network from the field. There are many types of portables with varying degrees of portability. One type in reality should be classified as "luggable." These are full-capacity computers with all the features of many of the stay-at-home models, but are less expensive, lighter, more compact, and come with a carrying handle. Since they weigh about thirty to forty pounds, however, they are not something you are going to want to throw on the front seat of your car every time you go out on a job.

If you want a computer that you are going to take out in the field, consider either a briefcase or a hand-held, pocket type. These are not full-featured computers. They are built to be small and handle a minimum amount of data. The usual built-in software includes an appointment scheduler, a simple word processor, and *BASIC* (a programming language). Plus, many now have built-in modems for data transmission over the telephone. If you travel and want to be able to call into an on-line network to get your electronic mail or to see if anyone is looking for photographers in your area, these small computers are ideal. The word processing feature can be used for note-taking, but do realize that these computers are not suitable for heavy work, especially since they have very limited storage capacity. There are also some combination portable feature computers. The keyboard is designed as a portable to go with you into the field. Back home, it plugs back into big brother for the heavier work.

Because of their need to be small, portable computers are the testing ground for new technology. As the technology is perfected and made less expensive, manufacturers will begin using it on the smaller, full-featured systems. Two areas add bulk to a computer: the monitor and the mass storage medium.

The luggable portables use the standard CRT found on the stay-at-home models. They are relatively inexpensive, the technology has been perfected (it is the same tube used in your TV set), and they are easy to read, especially in low-light situations. Their disadvantage for portable use is that they are bulky, heavy, fragile, and use a lot of power.

The most popular display used in the briefcase or pocket models is the LCD, similar to the type used on your pocket calculator. These are inexpensive and easy to read (though not in low-light situations like your darkroom), and use very little power. Most uses of LCD have been limited to one-line displays or, at the most, eight-line displays.

There are other methods for displaying data in portable computers, but their success will depend on their size and weight, energy requirements, readability, manufacturing cost, and amount of data that can be displayed (twenty-four lines by eighty columns is the computer standard). The ELDs (*electroluminescense displays*) use a chemical and wire grid between two plates of glass, while gas plasma displays use gas instead of a chemical. Characters are formed by applying voltage to the correct series of wires. There has also been some success in the development of the flat CRTs, such as the tiny watchband TVs.

Floppy disks are still the least expensive, and therefore the most popular medium of storage used on many portables. Either the standard 5¼ diskette or the microfloppy is used. A few portables use hard disks. To minimize the head crash problem, they have developed special shock mountings and head positioning controls. But hard disk drives and disks are still heavy and bulky.

Bubble-memory cartridges have been around for a long time, but they are very expensive. They have no moving parts and no read/write head. Data are stored in patterns of magnetic bubbles that do not lose their charge when the power is shut off.

5.8

BUNDLING

The computer you choose for use at home or in the office will cost between three thousand and five thousand dollars. A full-featured luggable portable will probably run fifteen hundred to three thousand dollars. The problem with computers is that their cost does not stop with the hardware. That machine you buy needs very expensive software. You can expect to pay at least one thousand dollars or more just to get enough software to put you in business.

Many hardware manufacturers are now selling their computers *bundled;* that is, the computer comes complete with most of the software you will ever need. Usually this includes BASIC, a word processor, a file manager, a spreadsheet, and some other goodies—all free. One disadvantage to this is that you really don't have any choice as to what software you will be getting. But when it is free, you will be amazed how much you can make it do. Also, as a beginner, you will find it hard to make software judgments until you have used some. Even if you eventually change your mind and decide you want to purchase a particular software package not furnished with the computer, you have had the advantage of working with software to discover what you do and do not like about it.

Along with your computer, you will probably get some software for which you really have no use. But since it's free, maybe someday you'll find it useful. You really can't beat the price on bundling, especially in a full-featured portable. Together you can get all the computer power you will probably ever want or need for less than half the price of a nonportable computer for which you have to purchase separate software.

5.9

WHAT SHOULD YOU BUY?

Now for the big question. What should you buy? Let's start with the basic computer. It should have at least 64K memory capacity. Most of the software in which you'll be interested operates effectively with this amount of memory. If you are interested in some of the fully integrated software, then consider a computer with more memory. Should you get an 8-bit, 16-bit, or 32-bit computer? I don't think it will make that much difference to you as long as the memory is adequate and the software you want will run on the machine.

The monitor and keyboards are personal choices—just follow the guidelines covered in the sections on those devices.

What about disk drives? You will need at least two of these—one for software and one for data. You will also need two so you can back up your disks for data security. Your disk drive should also be able to read at least a double-density, single-sided, 5¼-inch disk. This will serve most of your applications. If, however, you want to use larger, integrated software packages, or a thesaurus or other large dictionary—or do not want to spend a lot of time changing disks—then you will want to get larger-capacity disks. Your budget and needs will dictate your decision. If you do get a hard disk such as a Winchester, you will need at least one floppy disk drive to back up your nonremovable Winchester disk and to introduce new software, since software is usually sold on floppy disks. Also, if you will be sending text material in electronic form—say, to a publisher—you will probably need a floppy disk.

How about printers? If you have the money and don't mind the slow speed, a letter-quality printer might be nicer. If you will be doing a great deal of printing but have a limited budget, get a high-quality matrix printer. Avoid the cheap models. Make sure the printer will accept friction-fed 8½x11-inch paper and will print normal typewriter-size characters.

Your computer should come with at least one parallel and one serial interface so that you can plug in your printer and possibly a modem. The serial plug should be the standard RS-232 type.

If you can get a computer that comes with free software, consider that to be a big bonus and a money saver. The vendor has made some good choices for you. This software should include a word processor, a file management system (including mail generator), and a spreadsheet.

When you price the computer system, make sure the price comparison includes all the hardware and software you think you'll need.

5.10

WHERE TO BUY A COMPUTER

No matter where you decide to buy a computer, the best place to both buy and to start looking is at a computer store. Computers are usually sold at full retail price at these stores, but do shop around. Some give discounts or have specials. If this is your first computer, try to find a store that gives you support after you have purchased the computer. You will find this both indispensable for the first few weeks you have the computer, and reassuring as time goes on.

Just as mail-order photography equipment is available through the ads in the backs of photography magazines, so computer equipment and software can be purchased through ads in computer magazines. Equipment and software will generally be less expensive when ordered this way, but you will not get any support. If you are just starting out with computers, pay the premium and purchase through a dealer who will give you some support. If you are a seasoned computer user and don't need help, by all means look for a bargain. Shop around for the best buy in computer supplies, such as printer ribbons and diskettes.

Computer rentals are about as hard to find as camera rentals. They do exist, though, and if you can find one that carries the computer in which you are interested, it may be a good way to try out a computer before purchasing it. In the long run, you will probably prefer to purchase your own computer, since renting can be expensive. But if you find yourself in fast-changing business situations, if your accountant thinks there is a tax advantage to renting or leasing a computer, or if the computer you own breaks down and can't be fixed for a month, remember that renting is an option.

Since computers are such a new market, used computers are hard to find. But just as people trade in or sell their old cameras, so will people start selling their old computers. A used computer can be a very good buy, provided software is still available for it and it hasn't been dunked in the swimming pool. There is very little that can go wrong with a computer. The most vulnerable parts are the mechanical components like the disk drives. If the disk drives are no good but the used computer is a bargain, merely replace the disk drives. Be certain that it is not a discontinued model and that the original manufacturer of the computer or the peripherals is still in business. Otherwise it may be very hard to get parts for it if something should go wrong.

If you are buying your computer through a dealer, try to get some sort of warranty on it. If you are buying from an individual, try to find out why that person is selling the computer. Many people sell their computers because they are upgrading to another model and there is probably nothing wrong with the computer. Many people who have bought computers become discouraged with or can't find a use for them. These computers are as good as new. If they are not selling the computer for one of those reasons, be cautious. They may be selling it because they've had problems that they are not telling you about. Ask if you can take it to a computer repair shop and have some diagnostic tests run on it. If you do find a used computer that does everything you want it to do, it may be the least expensive way to go.

6

EVALUATING SOFTWARE

Perfect software does not exist, at least not yet, so your choices must depend on compromise. Fortunately, the software you choose for your business does not have to be the "ultimate" software product. The only problem you might have is knowing, at this particular point, what features you truly do need. Some features, though, will be obvious to you. Unless you write scholarly books, you probably don't care if your word processor handles footnoting. More important, you will want to evaluate the software in terms of its ease of use, the quality of the instructional manual that accompanies it, its compatibility with other software you might want to use, and whether it is a product that has been in use for some time.

Since humans do make mistakes and software is developed by human programmers, the software you choose will undoubtedly have some processing faults, usually referred to as "bugs." No matter how well a programmer tests the software to shake out the bugs, it usually takes the efforts of an undisciplined user to find the really pesky creatures. For that reason, never be the first one on your block to use a new piece of software. Let someone else break it in first. After some heavy use, many of the bugs will be located. The software vendor will probably issue a new and improved version or a "patch" to the old. You will still encounter bugs, but the worst will be gone.

6.1

DOCUMENTATION

When you evaluate software, be sure to also evaluate the instructions ("documentation") that come with it. The software vendor puts a lot of time and effort into the presentation of this documentation; it looks very readable and easy to use. But don't be fooled by appearances. Quite often very little time and effort was put into its actual *preparation.* When you do get into the documentation and start using it, you may find the instructions unclear or difficult to follow. You may find information missing, and even some that is totally wrong. If the vendor's documentation is poor, check to see if your bookstore carries a book on the software that might be better. If you cant find decent documentation, count that as a big negative factor against the software. You will rely on the documentation to help you use the software, so no matter how good the software might be, it is of no value to you if you can't figure out how to use it.

How do you judge documentation when it looks well presented and simple? Try it out at your computer store. Don't let the salesman do it for you or show you how. Pick something at random out of the documentation and see if you can follow the instructions by actually doing it on the computer. This is also an excellent way to try out the software.

Sometimes you'll find internal documentation within the system which you can refer to on your screen while you are actually using the software. This is called simply "help." It is only meant to be a memory aid. The main advantage is that it is readily available and you don't have to rummage through a book just to clarify a command.

Some software comes with reference cards or templates that fit over the keyboard and serve the same purpose as the help option. If your software doesn't have these, don't worry about it. You can always make up your own summary cards, which may be even better suited to you.

The term *documentation* as used in the computer world refers to anything written about the product. It can be technical or instructional. You will be interested in three types: *user manuals*, which tell you how to use the system; *tutorials*, which give some practical applications to try out with specific instructions on how to do each step; and a *reference manual* to use, after you have learned the system, to refresh your memory on certain terms.

Some software packages come with lesson disks, or these disks can be purchased from another company for the more popular software products. Like the tutorials, they lead you through some typical applications of the software product but do it directly on your screen. This way you can actually practice and learn how to use the software without having to constantly refer to a book. Some may even recognize when you have made an error and will tell you the correct response.

6.2

SOFTWARE COMMANDS

There are many different techniques for communicating with software. Some are easy to use but are slow. Others are quick but a little harder for you to learn.

Menus are often used to guide the uninitiated through the software functions. A menu is a list of options available, spelled out in plain English. It is quite similar to the menu you use in a restaurant. You merely select the option you want from the menu, which in turn may lead to an action or to another menu.

Another method of communicating with software is the *question-and-answer* approach. The computer will ask you a series of questions to be answered with a simple yes or no. Or it may ask you for some specific information, such as a file name, that you must provide before it can proceed.

A slightly faster method is the use of *keywords*. These are special, reserved commands to which the software has been programmed to respond in a set way. You do have to memorize these keywords, and for speed, they are often code words. However, there are usually only a few; plus, an on-screen "help" option or a reference card can make the process quite simple to use.

An even faster way of instructing software is to use combination keys or *function* keys. These are reserved to perform certain operations. They are often labeled on your keyboard as F1, F2, and so on, or they may be labeled with the specific operation they are intended to perform. The F-type keys are more flexible, since they are defined by the software in use at the time, and each type of software will have a unique set of functions. Needless to say, you will need a keyboard designed with those function keys in place if you are going to be able to use function keys. However, sometimes the ten-key numeric pad, available on many keyboards or any other unused keys, can be used as function keys. You can purchase special software that will convert any keys to any specific function you need. If your software does use function keys, make sure it provides you with a "help" option to tell you the purpose of each key. As you move from software product to software product, you may not remember what each key was intended to do.

With combination keys, a function key is used in combination with another keyboard key, usually a letter. The function keys used are standard on any computer keyboard and are usually the conveniently located Control (CTRL) and Escape (ESC) keys. Some attempt is usually made to choose keyboard keys that prompt the action. For instance, a *CTRL-E* may mean *enter data*, a *CTRL-D* may mean *delete*, or an *ESC-?* may mean you need instructions to help you.

There is some debate over which is better, the combination keys or the function keys. If you are just learning a software product, the function key is definitely easier to learn. However, if the product requires regular typing and speed, as with word processors, the combination key would probably be better in the long run. Function keys are located off the keyboard, so you have to interrupt your activity to find the proper function key. Combination keys can be used without moving your fingers off the keyboard.

The software industry is getting quite imaginative in its people/computer communications. You will hear of a gadget called a *mouse*. This is a device that is rolled along a pad or desktop. Its position on the pad or desktop corresponds to the position of the cursor on the screen. A device similar to the mouse is a *touch panel*. It works the same way as a mouse, but you position the cursor by moving your finger on the pad. Most often these methods are used with *icons*. An icon is merely a symbol of the action that you want to do. Instead of issuing a command to delete a record, you move the cursor to a picture of a piece of paper being thrown in a wastebasket. This is "user-friendly" for the illiterate.

In reality, many of the above techniques are used in combination. Practice with the software in your computer store and see how the software leads you through each operation. Then evaluate the commands used in terms of how much you will actually be using the system.

6.3

UTILITY SOFTWARE

You will not use utility software in your business applications, but utility programs are very important in using your computer system. Utility programs allow you to communicate with your hardware devices, to use other software, or to customize your system. They are, however, very machine oriented. The commands may be difficult for you to understand at first. Fortunately, most of what they do will be transparent to you; there are few commands that you will actually have to learn to use.

6.3.1 Operating Systems

Probably the most important utility software you will use is your operating system. In fact, you cannot run your computer without an operating system. Other software is written to be compatible with a certain operating system, and a particular microprocessor may be supported by only one operating system. So if your heart is set on using one particular piece of software, that choice may predetermine what operating system you must use and what computer you must buy. The real conflict is when you must also have another piece of software but it is for another operating system and consequently for a different computer. That is why the emphasis of this book is on evaluating your needs first and then looking at all your software requirements. Your individual software choices may not be optimal, but collectively they should be able to do everything you expect from a system.

Actually, there are only a limited number of operating systems you should be considering for your business. The CP/M-80 operating system for 8-bit computers, used by more different types of computer systems than any of the others, has become the standard. And, of course, a great deal of software has been written to work with this operating system. Much software has also been written for both the Apple-DOS operating system that runs the Apple computers and their look-alikes, and for the TRS-DOS operating system that runs the Radio Shack computers. CP/M will also run on these computers.

It is hard to tell what operating system will emerge as the leader with the 16-bit machines. Both the CP/M-86 and MS-DOS operating systems have received strong support from software developers. MS-DOS is also known as PC-DOS, the chosen operating system for the IBM Personal Computer. Many machines are supported by both operating systems, so you have a great deal of flexibility here.

You will hear of other operating systems, but right now, only consider those mentioned above. A lot of software has been and will be written for them. Even if a fantastic new operating system is developed, it will take a little time for the software market to catch up. Stick with the tried and true.

Not only do operating systems manage communications among the microprocessor, other software, and other hardware, but they also provide many utility programs that will help you with your general housekeeping. There will be utility programs to format your disks, to copy files, and to give you information on disk contents, such as how much room files take up or how much room is left on a disk. Operating systems utilities will display or print the contents of a file, and will even let you delete or rename files. Your operating system will also probably have a *text editor*, a primitive word processor. If you have a word processor, you will never use the text editor; if you don't have a word processor, the text editor is better than nothing. It will create data files, make corrections, and search for data items. It is not fancy, and since it is very machine oriented, you may find it difficult to understand. But you can use the text editor to write programs and do limited word processing.

6.3.2 Other Utilities

If you are going to be using Photonet, Photo-1, or any other on-line network, you must get a modem plus communications software that works with the modem. The communications software is the interface between the microprocessor, the modem, and the phone line. It controls the transmission speed, checks for errors in the data transmission, and originates or answers communications. These software products, as well as the on-line networks, will be covered in Chapter 10, The Photo Networks.

If you will be using data from other computing systems, you may need a utility that converts the format of one disk to the format used by your system. There are, however, other ways around this problem. You can cable the two computers together through your serial port or, if the computers are some distance from one another, transmit the data via your telephone line through your communication system.

One final utility you might want to consider is one that can redefine your keyboard keys so that you can change some of your unused keys to function or foreign-language keys. Sometimes this can be accomplished through your operating system, but the special utilities will be easier for you to use.

6.4 GENERALIZED SOFTWARE

Generalized software includes word processors, data management systems, financial management systems, and their related support systems. These can be looked at separately or as a total package. Unfortunately, when approaching them as a package, one part of the package may be a very good piece of software, while another piece is just terrible. On the other hand, if you choose the best of each type separately, they may be incompatible with each other. There are some definite advantages in having each system able to work with the others. But until there is better software, you will have to make compromises.

If you are going to consider generalized software packages, be prepared to put in a great deal of time learning to use them. These packages are not specific like special-applications software. They are designed to be tools, which work through your creativity. But in order to give you the most flexibility, they must have a fairly comprehensive set of instructions for you, which you must learn. The more you know, the more useful the software will be to you. You will also find yourself being more creative in the way you use it. Learning to use it, though, is like learning a foreign language or playing the piano. It isn't too difficult to learn enough phrases to order dinner in another country or to play a simple tune, but it takes a lot of time and practice to actually become proficient. When you first look at the generalized packages, you may be a little overwhelmed and discouraged. Don't be. Evaluate them in terms of what they can potentially do and then commit yourself to learning how to use them.

6.4.1 Word Processing

Just about every word processor on the market will fit your needs as a photographer. The differences between word processing systems are really minor, and some of the extras offered are not really important to you unless you also happen to be preparing your doctoral thesis.

Word processor features can be broken into four types: *informational, edit, print formatting,* and *utility.* Within each, some features are necessary, some are useful, some are handy to have, and some you will never use. You may even find new uses for some.

6.4.1.1 Informational Features

A menu-driven word processor will be easier to use initially, especially when you are faced with an almost overwhelming number of commands you must use. A convenient feature is the ability to ask for help. If you don't remember how to do something, it is handy if the system can prompt you right on the screen.

Screen information in edit mode (when you are working with text) can be important. One useful feature is to know where the page breaks are going to be on your final printed copy. Let's say you are writing a letter and you don't know where the page will end. Remember, your screen length does not correspond to the length of a printed page. When you print it, you discover that the body of the letter fits on one page but the word "Sincerely" is on the next page all by itself. You can fix it and reprint it, but you will have wasted time and paper. Also, the screen should show you which file you are working on, if you are in any special mode, and when you have made an error. The error message should also be accompanied by a buzzer to get your attention.

If you need to list items in columns, it is handy to have an option of either displaying the tab locations or at least having the software tell you in what column your cursor is located. Sometimes your text can be quite long, so when you print it you may want to make sure you have enough paper in the printer. You can estimate this if your word processor tells you how many lines of text you have or how many characters are in your text file. Most systems will allow you to preview your printed output by displaying it on the monitor in its final printed format.

6.4.1.2 Text Editing

Your monitor screen will probably display 80 characters of text across and 24 lines down. Your text will probably be longer than those 24 lines. To your computer, your text is just one continuous file. Think of that text as being printed on a long single sheet of paper. Your screen is actually a window that allows you to look at sections of that continous sheet of paper. That sheet is moved up or down as you move through the text. This is called *scrolling*. A word processor handles this situation in two ways. One is to simply display sections of the text as single short pages. Another is to *roll* the text up on the screen, line by line. Whichever you choose is entirely a matter of preference. Try out both methods at your computer store to see which you like.

One of the most important features in a word processor is automatic wraparound or *fill*. As you type a string of words and you come to the end of the line, the word processor evaluates the length of the line to best set the right margin, and your string of words automatically continues on the next line. You don't have to worry about the end of the line, margins, or carriage returns. If you will be doing any work on the word processor that requires you to put text into all eighty columns, it is equally important to be able to turn off the fill mode.

In a word processor, your position in the text is marked by a cursor. By moving it around, you can get to other portions of your text. Your word processor should have the following cursor movements: backward and forward letter by letter, line by line, word by word, sentence by sentence, paragraph by paragraph, and from the beginning to the end of the document. The deletion instructions should follow the same pattern: forward and backward by letter, word, line, sentence, paragraph, and marked region.

One important feature, not always found in all word processors, is the ability to retrieve deleted data. You may purposely delete data and then change your mind, or worse, inadvertently delete data and not remember what they were. If you are deleting data to be inserted into another portion of your text, this retrieval function is very important. Some systems will only let you delete one block of data and still be able to retrieve it, and another deletion overwrites the previous one. If you think your particular work is going to require a lot of revision, you'll want to find out if the software will let you collect successively deleted text and then retrieve all of it in another part of your text.

Some word processors allow correction by overwriting. That is, you just type over the old text, and it is replaced by the new. This is not the preferred way. It is better if whatever you type is inserted in the text at the location of the cursor. As the new characters are inserted, the characters already in your text are pushed to the right, and this causes them to travel around your lines. If this makes you a little seasick, make sure your word processor allows you to open up the text before making insertions.

As you add and delete text, your paragraphs might start looking pretty ragged. Most word processors allow these paragraphs to be reformatted in the printing. If, however, you are printing the text as formatted on the screen or find this psychologically disturbing, look for a feature in your word processor that automatically reformats your paragraphs.

Probably one of the most useful commands is the *search* command. Whether you are writing a letter or have decided to put the New York telephone directory on your word processing system, this command will allow you to search for any combination of characters at electronic speeds. The search-and-replace instructions can also help you make changes throughout your entire text. If you want to change all "ASA" references to "ISO," you merely indicate that you want "ASA" to be replaced by "ISO." The computer will then search out every occurrence of the word and make the change for you. The computer, however, is unthinking in its substitution and obeys your commands literally. If, for instance, you decide to change all your "you's" to "I's," your dumb computer will make all the changes but leave you with some very strange verbs and equally strange uses of the word "I." So make sure your word processing system lets you monitor the changes and interrupt the process with your own corrections.

A feature that you may not use immediately but may find invaluable later is the ability to use multiple files and to transfer data between those files. A particularly nice enhancement is the ability to view both files at the same time by splitting the screen. I use mine in several ways. For example, I keep an electronic notebook on a file. When I am writing, I can split my screen and refer to the notebook as I write. If my notebook contains an inspirational paragraph, I can easily transfer it over. I also keep a list of addresses to which I frequently write. When I start a letter, I call up my address file, search automatically for the appropriate name, and transfer the address onto my letter file.

The ability to do arithmetic is not found on too many word processing systems. If you are preparing a bill or a job quote, it would be handy if your word processor could also add up the figures for you.

6.4.1.3 Print Format Instructions

Format instructions tell your computer how to print your text. Some word processing software will format your text into groups with special spacing and indentations. It will even number items for you, or highlight items with a special character. This leaves you free to type your text without stopping to do any special tabbing or spacing. It is, however, very important that your word processor can print your text exactly as it appears on the screen. As long as it can do that, many of the format instructions are handy but not necessary.

Your word processing software should enable you to change the size of the margins and be able to at least double-space and single-space. You may be given the option of having the right margin justified by proportionally spacing your text across the line. If you like the look of straight margins, you might put that on your list. Your word processor should also handle page numbering for you. A section heading could end up at the bottom of a page when the page is printed; naturally, you would prefer it to be at the top of the next page, so you would want the ability to force the beginning of a new page.

Your word processor will probably let you underline text and print in boldface or even in italics, but these are of little value unless your printer can also carry out these operations. So if these options are important to you, don't forget to make sure the printer you select will handle them.

6.4.1.4 Word Processing Utilities

The main utilities provided by the word processing system are reading and writing disk files and printing your text file. Everything else is available through your operating system. However, some of these operating system functions are useful to have directly through the word processing system. Most systems allow you to write your text to a file name different from the one you originally designated. This is important if you should have some disk problems and need to write your text to a new file name or if you want to save the original, unchanged text. As you will learn later, you must save extra copies of your text in case some damage is done to the disk. This procedure is called "backing up." Some systems will do the backup for you automatically. This is handy if you are not very good about remembering to backup your files, but it does reduce your available disk space by one-half. Another useful option for forgetful folks is to have the system automatically save the working file on disk after a certain number of characters has been keyed in.

Other features that are nice to have in the word processor mode—but not necessary—are the ability to look at the disk directory, delete a file, or rename a file.

6.4.2 Word Processing Support Systems

Some word processing software comes with extra features that check your spelling, grammar, and word usage. If your word processing system does not have these features or if you are not satisfied with the way these features work in your particular system, you can obtain them as separate software.

The most popular word processing system extra is the spelling checkers. This takes each unique word in your text and compares it against its own dictionary. If the spelling of a word does not match that in the dictionary, then it is flagged as a possible misspelling. Since some spelling checkers just check word roots to keep down the size of the dictionary, some misspellings can slip through such checkers. The better ones check full words but will flag a lot of correctly spelled words, such as plurals. Many of the photographic terms you frequently use might not be in the main dictionary, and they will be flagged every time. It is better if the spelling checker allows you to put your own words into its dictionary or a special dictionary, to avoid having your unique words show up as errors every time you run your text through the spelling checker.

Most dictionaries will mark the offending word in your text with a special character. You then use the search capabilities of your word processor to find the marked words so that you can correct them. The better checkers make the corrections for you. This is especially helpful if you use the word frequently, since the checker will correct all occurrences of the word. Better still are the spelling checkers that look up the correct spelling of the word for you. Most people tend to misspell words in consistent ways. By using these rules, the spelling checker will search its dictionary for correct versions of your words.

If you are a creative speller, you can sometimes find one other feature; you can give the checker whatever letters you are sure of and ask the checker to search its dictionary for any words that match that criteria. It's also great for doing crossword puzzles! Scrabble and anagram fans may find some handy features in these spelling checkers, as may poets looking for rhymes. Some other extras you writers might find useful are word-counting capabilities, and the ability to let you know how frequently you use particular words.

6.4.3 Data Management Systems

There are two types of data management systems, though the distinction should become less evident as new software is developed. The first is the *file management system*, and the second is the *data base system*.

The file management system is easier to use but is less flexible than the database system. The information you want to keep is stored in *fields* in individual records in a particular file, not unlike your paper files. A client file will contain individual records for each client.

A data base system is less structured than a file management system, eliminating much redundant data. It is, however, more expensive, harder to implement, and requires the use of a semiprogramming language, so it takes longer to learn. Unless you are ready to devote a lot of time to the project, stay with the easier file management systems.

DATA BASE SYSTEM: PORTION OF TRAVEL PHOTO FILE SHOWING SEARCH RELATIONSHIPS

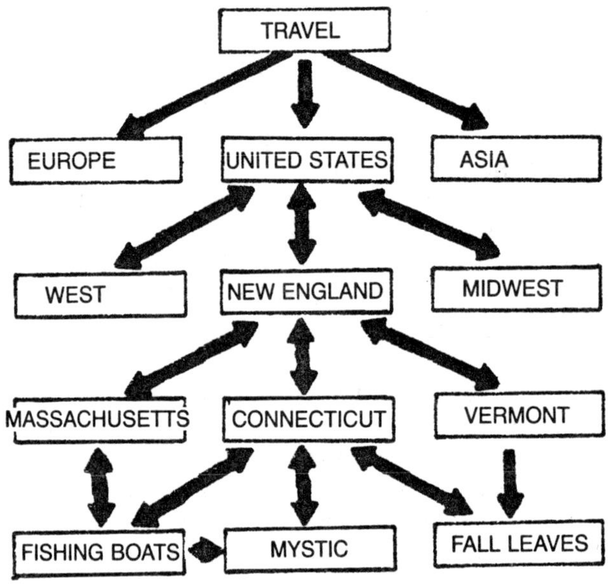

FILE MANAGEMENT RECORDS FOR CLIENT FILE

	Field	Field	Field	Field	Field	Field
Record 1	No	Client Name	Address	City	St	Zip
Record 2	No	Client Name	Address	City	St	Zip
Record 3	No	Client Name	Address	City	St	Zip
Record 4	No	Client Name	Address	City	St	Zip
Record 5	No	Client Name	Address	City	St	Zip

6-A. Data Base and File Management Systems

There is a lot of confusion in the terminology used to identify these software products, since they are called many different names. The term *data base* may be used to encompass all types of data management systems. Look beyond the terminology and evaluate the software by how easy it is for you to define your data requirements and use the system. How the software actually accomplishes the task is of no importance to you.

The system you choose should let you define your own data requirements and the manner in which you want to access them. Some systems let you draw your requirements on the computer screen in the actual form that you would like to see them. Others will format the screen for you, usually allowing one line per data item. Both types of systems will let you define your own *prompts*, the words that will appear on the screen to tell you what data to enter. Some may allow you to define any sort of prompt that is meaningful to you. Others might be very stingy in the number of characters you can use. Any file management system should allow you to add records to your file, to retrieve them as you have specified, to delete records you no longer need, and to change particular fields. Changes to fields can be made in two ways: either by moving the cursor from field to field or by selecting a field to be changed. The cursor method is better if you make many changes to a record but is slow if you have to move down to a field at the end of the record. The selection process is faster if you are only changing one or two fields but very slow if you are making many changes.

When evaluating file management software, make sure you understand how the software retrieves records. When you set up your file definition, you will designate a field or fields as the access key. The key is what you will use to retrieve the record. Some systems may limit your key definition, such as to a 4-character key or a single-key field. If you are going to retrieve your clients by a client number, this may be satisfactory. However, if you want to use a name field or retrieve that record on the basis of different criteria, then that limited method will not be suitable for your needs.

It is easier to use the system if you can define *defaults;* that is, predetermined values that are automatically put into a field if you don't put anything else in. For instance, if your client file has a code designating *active* or *inactive*, initially you would want all your entries to default to active. Some systems will let you copy forward data from one record to another. Let's say you are entering several clients from New York. Typing in "New York" once and being able to copy that information into successive records can save you a lot of time as well as errors.

Edit checking can reduce input errors if the system allows you to set up rules about what are valid data for a given field, and then compare your input against those rules to check for errors. These edit checks can include the following:

- *Type of Data:* Data can be defined as only *alphabetic data* (such as a code), only *numeric data* (such as ZIP code), or a combination called *alphanumeric* (street address).
- *Valid Codes:* The data may be limited to certain valid codes such as "A" for active or "I" for inactive.
- *Table Values:* You may have data that can be validated against a table of allowable values, such as validating states against a table of acceptable state code abbreviations.
- *Range Checks:* A common input error is to inadvertently add an extra character. A range check can catch some of these errors. Let's say the highest price you will charge for one of your pictures is two thousand dollars, so you set that as your upper range. If you sell a picture for five hundred dollars but accidentally enter the amount of five thousand dollars, the system will catch the error.

In most file management systems, you must call up each individual record to make changes. Very few systems have a feature called *batch processing*, which allows you to input all changes as individual transactions. The system reads in all those transactions and makes all changes to the individual records for you. Batch processing is far more efficient if you are making a lot of similar changes in many records. Let's say you have set up an accounting system to keep track of your income and expenses. It would take a long time to call up each income and expense record and to add in the new items; it would be difficult to detect an error when the updating is done this way. In batch processing, you would only have to input the key and the amount. Before the processing is done, the total amount could be verified (called *batch balancing)*, and then the system could update the appropriate records with those transactions while you go have a cup of coffee.

Until you have more experience in setting up file systems, chances are that you'll want to make modifications in the first one you set up after you have begun using it. The system you choose should allow such changes and, more important, should either retain or allow a conversion of your old data to the new record. Otherwise, you will have the big clerical job of inputting again all that data from the old file.

Most important of all, make sure that whatever system you do choose will interface with your word processing system. If there is only one that works with your word processing system and it is inadequate, you may have to consider two systems: one for your mail correspondence files that will work with your word processor and a better one for handling other filing needs, such as locating your photos.

6.4.4 Data Management Support Systems

Most of the newer data management systems come complete with all the support systems, since without them an information system has very limited value. But for some, each piece has to be purchased separately. If your system does not come with these support systems, make sure you can get a compatible system that can do the job.

One of the most useful systems is the mail generator. This is where the word processor and file management system get together to put out truly automated mass mailings. You prepare a form letter with the word processor, tagging the data elements to be inserted into the text. Your addresses and other information are in the file management system. The mail generator brings them together as a single letter. A nice feature is the ability to insert items from the file into the text of the letter or to have it stop to let you enter something from the keyboard so the letter seems more personalized. You should be able to print letters for your entire file, for certain groups (such as calendar companies), and for selected individuals.

Another useful feature that may or may not come with the base file management system is a *sort* capability. You should be able to designate which fields in your record are to be sorted, with the mail, labels, or reports coming out in the order you specify.

There will be times when you will want to list selective records and data from your files. For this you will need a *report generator*. You should be able to design both the report and the headings. You will want to select records on the basis of a certain criteria or to group records with like criteria. The generated program should take care of all paging. Counting and totaling capabilities would be other handy features.

A system that allows you to design your own output formats is helpful if you are using special preprinted forms or customized mailing labels. You should be able to define the size and the dimensions of the form to the printer. There should also be some way, probably through your word processor, for you to indicate the location of the data elements on the form.

6.4.5 Financial Management Systems

Financial management software is popularly known as spreadsheets, though some products may go far beyond the spreadsheet concept. As mentioned in Chapter 2, a spreadsheet is, conceptually, the same thing as an accountant's worksheet. More people use spreadsheet software than any other single type of software product. There are many spreadsheet software products available for virtually any machine. People are using them in ways never even envisioned by their inventors. Nonetheless, I have placed it third in your trio of generalized products because, as a photographer, you will only use it for bookkeeping and a few other less vital projects.

6.4.5.1 Format

The easiest way to think about spreadsheets is to put an accounting worksheet in front of you. Across the top of the sheet are the columns to identify the vertical data. Down the left-hand side of the worksheet are the rows which identify the horizontal data. The intersection

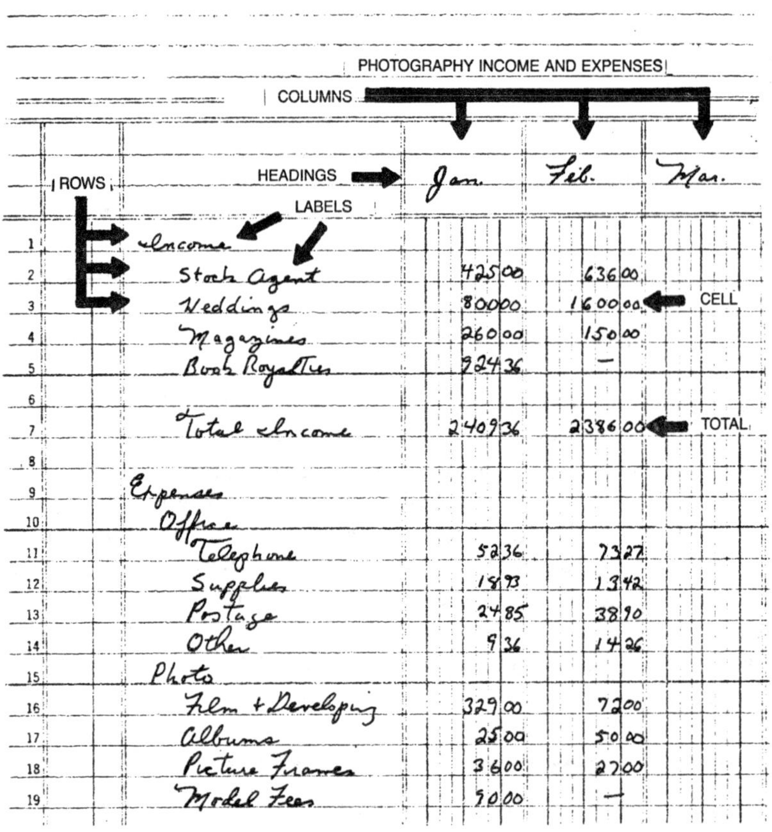

6-B. Accounting Worksheet

of the rows and columns is called a "cell." Typically, an electronic spreadsheet allows you sixty-four columns and 255 rows, though there is a great deal of variation. Some provide more columns than rows, some may give you only thirteen columns, and others may only limit the number of rows and columns to the capacity of your disk. Your choice depends, again, on the way you'll be using the spreadsheet. If you are going to use it to project your financial situation for the next three years, you will want to designate the columns as months. So a spreadsheet that gives you only thirteen columns will not accommodate the thirty-six months that you need. If, on the other hand, you are going to use the spreadsheet to post your mileage each day, you may not care how many columns are available but will want to make sure there are enough rows. If you use your car every day, that would mean at least 365 rows.

You'll need to be able to modify the width of the columns. Some spreadsheets also let you modify the height of the rows, though you will rarely need to do this. You will, however, want to change the width of the columns to be able to put in adequate descriptions for both the columns and rows. Check the ease of setting up these headings. Will the software center things for you, copy data forward to other headings, and let you change the headings easily?

One very important feature to look for in spreadsheet software is the ability to work on more than one spreadsheet at a time and to transfer data from one to another. The most important part of this feature is being able to view both spreadsheets on the screen at the same time. Splitting the screen horizontally gives a row-by-row comparison of information. Splitting the screen vertically shows column-by-column comparisons. Actually, this split-screen capability will be most important to you within a single file.

In the word processing section, you had to envision your text as a long, continuous piece of paper. Now think of your 64-column/255-row spreadsheet as a huge mural on your wall. You still have to view it through your 80-character by 24-line "window." As long as you are looking at the upper left-hand corner of your spreadsheet, you will not have any problems knowing what the column and row headings are. Farther away from the top and left-hand edge, you are in the middle of a bunch of unlabeled numbers. If you split your screen, you can put your headings in one portion and move around in your sheet in the other.

Setting up a spreadsheet can be a time-consuming task. However, many of the applications are fairly straightforward, like preparing tax forms or balancing a checkbook. Check to see if the spreadsheet package comes with some spreadsheet forms already set up for you to use.

6.4.5.2 Functions

As in the word processing system, you have to be able to move

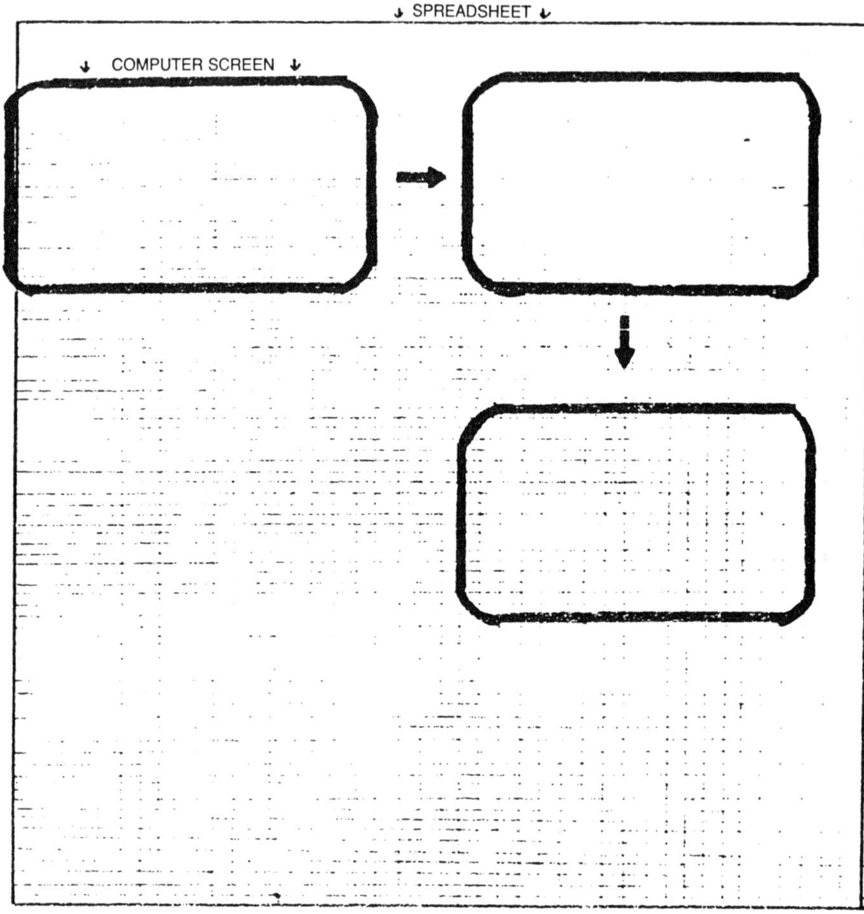

6-C. Spreadsheet Windows

your spreadsheet around, which is accomplished by moving the cursor. You should be able to move from cell to cell, column by column, and row by row, but you'll want to move around faster than that. You should have the ability to move directly to a cell (by row and column coordinates), to the top and bottom of the spreadsheet, and to the left- and right-hand margins. In your word processing system, your system had to scroll the text up; in your spreadsheet system, you will want to have the ability to scroll sideways as well.

Most spreadsheets have mathematical functions you will never want to use. The only one you will be concerned with are the basic arithmetic functions of adding, subtracting, multiplying, and dividing.

Spreadsheet arithmetic is done by identifying the cells by the column/row coordinates. Sometimes this is done by column/row labels, but most often the columns are identified by letters of the alphabet and the rows by numbers. So an item in column B and row (line) 25 would be identified as B25. If you wanted cell B25 to be the sum of cells B23 and B24, you would make up a formula for the B25 cell, such as B25 = B23 + B24. (Computers always do things backwards.) That is fine, but you may want to add up everything from row 1 to row 24. Since this may be a frequent need, make sure your spreadsheet allows you to reference groups of columns and rows and to perform the arithmetic on all items. Also, make sure it will move formulas and adjust them for different cells. You have that simple addition sample for column B, but you probably will want to do the same thing in column C. Then your formula would have to be C25 = C23 + C24. This can get to be pretty tedious if you have to do it for 36 columns. Make sure your software lets your computer do this work; it is much better suited to it than you are.

Another important function to look for is the ability to insert and delete columns and rows. Let's say you are setting up a spreadsheet to keep track of your daily expenses. You set up your columns for each day of the month. Your rows are the types of expenses you expect to incur during the month, grouped by category such as office, travel, photo supplies, and so on. You are halfway into the month when you discover that you forgot to put the item "postage" under the "office" heading. Now you want to put "postage" on row (line) 17. What happens to all those entries in row 18 and below? Worse, what about those formulas like B25 = B23 + B24? They will be addressing the wrong rows. Again, your computer can handle this tedious work better than you can, so make sure the software can handle these types of changes.

6.4.5.3 Output

You will want to be able to print your spreadsheet, but unless you own a printer that prints on mural-size paper, this may be a problem. Most spreadsheet software should make provisions for printing your spreadsheet one page at a time. The only thing you will really have to check is whether it prints your column and row headings on each page; otherwise, you will find yourself spreading each piece of paper on the floor and taping them all together.

It will be very helpful if your spreadsheet file can be used with your word processing system. This way you can clean up the spreadsheet layout any way you want to by using the edit functions of your word processing system. Let's say you have set up a spreadsheet to price certain assignments. Now you want to include those figures in a letter to your client. Instead of recopying all those numbers into your word processing system, you can pull in the spreadsheet and tidy it up a bit.

6.5

INTEGRATED SOFTWARE

The generalized application software described in the previous section can be purchased individually to solve a particular and isolated problem. For instance, you may only need a word processor to help you write travel articles, and you don't intend to use your computer for anything else. This is referred to as a *stand-alone* system. However, if you need to use several different types of software that should be able to interact with each other, then you are probably going to want to consider *integrated* software.

The only problem is that there is no clear definition of what "integrated" means, and there are many different solutions to the integration problems. First, let's look at some of the more popular definitions of integration.

- *All-In-One Package:* This actually has several definitions. It can simply be the packaging of several stand-alone systems on a single disk for convenience. Or it can be a single program that performs all the functions of word processing and file and financial management. And finally, it can be a single database that is used by several programs.
- *Operating Environment:* A special operating program can let you use the software products of different manufacturers together in a compatible working environment. The operating program controls the communications between the different software products. This approach gives you a great deal of flexibility.
- *Family Products:* One developer of software may actually set up the different products he markets so that they are compatible with each other. This usually means they all use similar commands and they can pass data between programs.
- *Hardware/Software Combinations:* Special-purpose computers have been designed to work with special software. These systems are usually easier to use because everything is compatible, but you are locked into the design features of the machine and software.

From your point of view, you only care if you can get the job done that you need to get done. If a stand-alone system does it for you, then that is all you need. If you use several systems, it is easier if they all share similar commands. If you find you are frequently changing disks, then it is nice if there is some compatible organization. (You can do this yourself, though. See the section "Configuring Your Files" in Chapter 9.) If you need to transfer data between programs or files, does your software let you do it, and in how many steps? Do you need to have some update function that applies all updates to all your files simultaneously?

And finally, for all this convenience, do you have the disk and memory capability to handle it, or are you willing to pay the extra money for it? Remember, something is not necessarily better because it does more, especially if you don't need to use it. Always look at software in terms of how you are going to use it.

6.6

SPECIAL APPLICATIONS SOFTWARE

If you find the right package, special applications software can be just great. All you have to do is to enter your data and start using the system. Unlike the general software where you have to design everything yourself, everything in the special applications software has been done for you. The main advantage of this type of software, however, is also its disadvantage. Everything has been done for you, and you have to do it that way. If you don't like the way it has been done or if it doesn't fit your business, don't bother with it.

The first thing to look at when evaluating special applications software is the reports and other output it generates. Does it give you what you want in the form you want it? Look at the screen information. Can you call up and check the information you need? Next, look at the type of data that are retained in the files. Do they have all the information you need, or will you have to maintain extra files apart from the system for additional information? If the reports or other output are inadequate, can you interface with the file, using your report generator, to get the output you need? How about the way data are entered into the system? Are you forced to enter a lot of data you don't need? Is it in a form totally different from the way you handle it now? Finally, can the system be customized without programming changes? For instance, some general ledger systems are driven by a "chart of account" table. You define your specific account needs, put in your own descriptions, and indicate how you want some accounts summarized or to what tax lines they are to be posted. This information is put into a table that directs the program instructions accordingly.

When looking at these packages, try to find the simplest system possible that can still take care of your needs. A home accounting system may take care of your business better than a full-fledged general ledger system. Look at these systems in terms of how they will specifically satisfy your business needs. Remember, they are usually not too flexible, so if you adopt one of these systems, your business will have to conform to it.

7

PUTTING IT ALL TOGETHER

If you have ever visited a major computer installation, you were probably awed by what was necessary to take care of the machine. The computer itself was in a specially built room with a raised floor necessary to cover all the cables. Air conditioning set at freezing temperatures kept the machine cool. You were probably also amazed at the number and types of people necessary to make sure the computer was doing what it was supposed to do. It needed operators day and night, data control clerks to check its output, and data entry clerks to prepare its input. System programmers were necessary to care for its operating system, maintenance programmers to repair the "bugs" in its programs, system analysts to design new applications for the computer, and applications programmers to convert those designs into instructions the computer could digest. Sometimes there were specialists in telecommunications, documentation, or data base management. All this for the use and benefit of a person who never saw or understood the machine—the user.

The personal computer does not require the special handling of its bigger relatives and certainly not the huge staff of human specialists. But all the same functions are still there. Now *you* have to be the operator, data entry and data control clerk, systems programmer, systems analyst, and maybe even the maintenance and applications programmer—as well as the user. You don't need the special training required of the technical staff in a big computer installation. But no matter what you were told at the computer store, your computer is not yet as simple as a toaster. You must become knowledgeable in the care and feeding of your computer.

7.1

THE WORKING ENVIRONMENT

Your personal computer really doesn't require much special care, but you should do a little planning for its physical environment. No special air conditioning is necessary. A rule of thumb is that if it is comfortable for you, it is comfortable for the computer. For you polar bear types or those of you who thrive in sauna conditions, this means a temperature of about fifteen to twenty-six degrees centigrade (or sixty to eighty degrees Fahrenheit) and a relative humidity of 20 percent to 80 percent. Too low a humidity could result in static electricity being discharged every time you walk across the carpet and touch the computer. If this is a problem, consider putting the computer on a tile floor or using an antistatic mat or spray.

Dust is probably the biggest problem you will ever have, so you should take some care to reduce the dust as much as possible. Put plastic covers over your computer and printer when not in use. Don't put your computer where there is a lot of traffic. Smoke can be as bad as dust, so it is best if you can keep smoke out of the area or at least away from the computer.

No special electrical requirements are necessary other than a ground plug. The only precaution is that no other major electrical appliances be located on the same circuit, such as your refrigerator or air conditioning unit. To be on the safe side, put a *surge protector* on your system. This device regulates the flow of electricity and can be purchased at any computer store. It is expensive but well worth the money. If there should be a spike in the power, as when a refrigerator goes off, or if the power should go off and come on again, your machine could be damaged if you do not have this protection.

Plan your computer area as you would any other business working space. Make sure there is a readily accessible place to store all your reference books and room to store computer paper and letterhead. You will need files for storing correspondence and computer printouts, plus a place to store diskettes. You'll find several types of diskette filing systems. In one system, the disks are stored in plastic envelopes in a notebook-type binder; another uses plastic boxes that hold ten disks each; still another holds twenty-five or more disks, with plastic dividers for easy filing.

Your computer can be used on a desk, but a desk designed for writing is not comfortable for typing. It is better to get furniture specifically designed for a computer or at least for typing. It need not be fancy—just the right height, which is about 25 to 26 inches (63 to 66 cm). Don't forget a decent chair. A steno chair with good back support will make those long hours at the keyboard less painful.

Arrange adequate lighting. An adjustable light that clips onto your desk works very well and doesn't take up much room. Make sure there is not a light or window directly behind you. Such a light source will reflect on the monitor screen and make working with the monitor difficult.

A telephone nearby is a definite convenience. Not only will you want it close enough so that you can talk to clients while consulting your computer, but in the early days of your installation, you'll want to be in contact with your salesperson as you learn your way through your system. If you have a modem, of course, the phone line will be a necessity; in fact, you may even need two.

7.2

MAKING THE PURCHASE

Finally, the day has arrived when you are ready to make your first trip to the computer store. You have decided you can use a computer, you know what a computer is and have learned some of the terminology, and you have a good idea of what you want in the way of software. You have done your research, and you know some specific computer systems, printers, and software that will do the job you need to have done.

Go to the Yellow Pages, look through the newspapers for ads, and write down every computer store. Mark those that specifically state that they have the computer or software in which you are interested. Then note the ones that appear to be big stores. Finally, mark the ones that are in your neighborhood. The marked stores are the ones you will be visiting. You will have to visit several stores, since most can carry and effectively demonstrate only a few types of machines and software. Also, you are shopping for a "home," a place where you feel comfortable and will want to revisit many times after the sale is made.

Because the purpose of your first visit is not to buy a computer but rather to get some hands-on contact with the machine and software, find out which stores have the software and hardware in which you're interested and evaluate those stores and their salespeople. Make your first visits *general.* You are there for some subjective learning. Don't ask to see a specific machine or software yet. Just tell the salespeople who greet you that you are a freelance photographer who needs a computer to keep track of your clients, to locate pictures, for bookkeeping, to use Photonet, and so on—whatever reasons have convinced you that you need a computer. Then see what the salespeople suggest and let them do a demonstration for you. Ask if you can try it yourself. This may be the first time you've even touched a keyboard. Don't be embarrassed if you are a hunt-and-peck typist—this is not a typing test. Do not be intimidated by the salespeople if they use words you don't understand. Just ask for a simple explanation. Remember that you are the customer, the one with the money, considering a possible five-thousand-dollar purchase. If questions do occur to you, ask them, but don't feel that you have to cover every point on the first visit or remember everything you were told. If they haven't shown you the software or hardware that interests you, ask if they have it, and if they do, ask for a demonstration. If you find that some of the software and equipment you were interested in doesn't seem to be in many stores, you might ask the salespeople why they don't stock it. Computer stores can only handle the most popular, best-selling products. They can get anything for you. But the reason they are not stocking it could be that it is too new (remember, you do not want to be the first one on the block), or it may just not be selling well (you don't want to purchase something from a company that is going to go out of business).

Collect all the brochures you can find, and, if you liked working with them, get the names of the salespeople. Take notes, including what machines and software the stores had that interested you, anything new you learned for your own later research, and which salespeople were helpful and seemed knowledgeable.

After you have completed your visits to all the stores on your list, you will find yourself a lot smarter. You will have a good idea of what software and equipment you like. You know what stores carry the products you are interested in, and you probably have the names of some salespeople with whom you would like to do business: Now it is time for your second round of visits.

Think about the specific questions you need to ask and write them down. Put together a sample application, with a couple of client files, some sample letters, or some receipts that you would enter into your accounting records. No need to make it comprehensive; just make sure it represents the things you will want to do with the computer.

The next time you go into the computer store, you will be specific. Ask to see a particular machine and specific software. Sit down at the keyboard yourself; don't let the salesperson do it for you. You are the one who is going to be taking it home. Try your sample application. Don't worry about taking up the salesperson's time—take all the time you need until you feel comfortable with the system. Ask if you can use it alone for a while; you will feel less pressure that way. If you have questions, write them down to ask the salesperson later, over the phone.

When you evaluate software and machines, make sure you keep them separate and distinct in your own mind. The software isn't defective just because the computer has a poorly designed keyboard; nor is the computer terrific because you like the software it uses. Evaluate the computer in terms of its physical attributes, and the software in terms of what it does and how easy it is to use. During your evaluation, try different software in the same machine and the same software in another machine.

Return to the store with additional applications. Shop around at other stores. If you arrive at a time when they are very busy, take the time to look over other people's shoulders and see what they are doing. If there is a customer who has dealt with the store, ask him about its support and service.

Now it is time for you to evaluate all the systems you have examined. If there are several systems you like, your decision will be based on cost. List all the prices and components of the system and all the software you'll need to start. Remember, you are buying a total package. Reread some of the software and hardware magazine reviews; they may mean more to you now. Talk to friends. Even if they don't know anything about computers, just talking might help.

You've come this far, and now there is one more nagging problem. Computers are getting cheaper, software is getting better, and you have read reviews of some hot new products. Should you buy now or wait? If you think you need a computer, then buy one. Even if the new product looks terrific, you don't want to be the person who breaks it in. Also, the computer industry has a bad habit of announcing products that are either never delivered or are not even in production yet. The announcements are intended to keep you from buying somebody else's product today and to wait for theirs, or the manufacturers may be testing the market to see if there is enough interest in their product before it goes into expensive production. Keep in mind that there will always be a better and cheaper product no matter when you decide to buy. Buy it now, depreciate it on your taxes, and when it is fully depreciated, go out and buy a new one.

You have finally made up your mind what software and hardware you want to purchase. The only question is, where? Remember to find out what kind of support the store is willing to give you. Will they show you how to set the machine up, give you some training on using the software, and be available to answer your questions? What if the machine breaks down? Will they replace it, be able to fix it—or will you have to wait a month or two while they send it back to the manufacturer? And don't forget that helpful salesperson. He or she is the one you are really going to be dealing with.

7.3

WHAT TO DO WHEN YOU GET THE COMPUTER HOME

Finally, the big day is here. You go to the computer store and purchase your computer system, printer, and software. Be sure to also purchase continuous-form paper and at least one box of blank diskettes. When you arrive at home or office, open up the boxes and take out the precious contents. Save the boxes and the packing material just in case you have to ship something back to the manufacturer. And don't forget to keep the receipts for that all-important tax deduction.

Don't be too anxious to get started. First take the time to look through the documentation that came with your computer and printer. Fill out all the warrantees and mail them. Then sit down with the installation manuals and read them first. Actually, installation is as easy as plugging in, but you might want to make sure there isn't any extra packing lurking about that you haven't noticed, and that all the proper things have been done before you turn on any power. Your printer might turn out to be the most difficult part of the installation, so read that manual carefully. There may be something called *dip switches* that have to be set, though your computer vendor should have set them for you. You will have to connect your printer to your computer with a cable. If you have a serial printer, it will have to connect to the serial port of your computer. If it is a parallel printer, it will have to connect to your parallel port. Actually, if you have the correct cable, there is only one plug and one direction that will work, so you really can't make a mistake.

Now you plug in the computer, turn it on, and of course it does nothing but tell you to put something in drive A. But before doing anything, there is a bit of housekeeping you must attend to first. Open up that box of blank diskettes you bought. Put your operating system into drive A and a blank disk into drive B. The first question you may ask is: How do I put a disk into a drive? If your drives are mounted horizontally, put the disks in so that the label on the disk faces up. If your drives are mounted vertically, insert the disks so the label faces the monitor.

As soon as you put your operating system into drive A, your system will come alive. This process is called *booting* the system. There is a program in the ROM (read-only memory) that reads the operating system into memory and then turns control over to the operating system. It is literally "pulling itself up by its own bootstraps." You can reboot your computer anytime by pushing the "reset" button.

Now follow your operating system's instructions for formatting your disk. (It is probably a simple command such as "format" or "copy blank.") An unformatted disk will not work in your computer, so each of

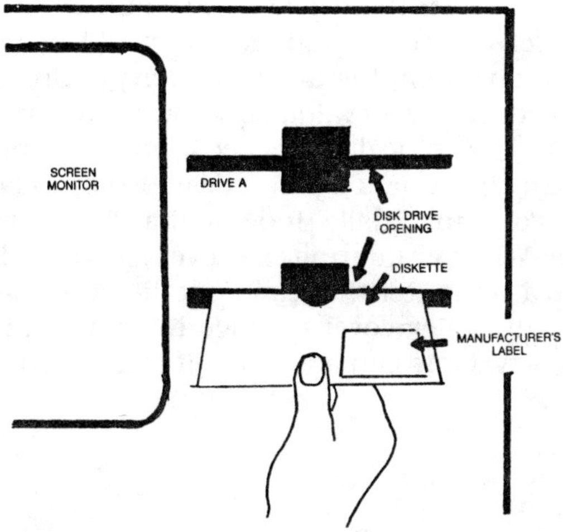

7-A. Inserting a Diskette

your disks must be formatted first. Whenever you buy new diskettes, it is a good idea to format them as soon as you get them home. Don't forget, or someday you will find yourself needing a disk and finding it unusable. After you format each disk, write a number on it. This way you will know it has been formatted, and it will have a unique identification.

Next, take out your master software disks and copy them one by one onto your newly formatted diskettes, again following the directions with your operating system (probably a command called "copy"). NEVER USE YOUR MASTER SOFTWARE DISKETTES—*always* make a copy first. Then store your master diskettes, preferably in a totally different location. Those masters, whether they came free with your system or not, are worth hundreds of dollars. Should something happen to your software, you may find yourself having to buy the software again.

After you copy the diskette, you will probably get a message from your operating system about copying the operating system onto the disk (probably referred to as SYSGEN). A copy of the operating system is necessary to boot the system when you use the software. Properly label each disk and store them in a dustproof box.

7.4

INSURANCE

Chances are that your homeowner's policy will not cover the loss of your computer, especially if it is used for business. If you have a business policy, it may be covered under that, or you may be able to get a floater to specifically cover the loss of your computer. This would include the physical loss or damage to your computer due to burglary or fire. The problem is that it may not cover your very valuable software. You are better off finding insurance that is specifically designed to cover computers. Ask your insurance company if it offers a policy designed especially for computers. If it doesn't, you can usually find one that does advertised in computer magazines. When evaluating the coverage, consider some of the things unique to a computer that can nonetheless cause you loss. For instance, does your policy cover damage to your computer due to a power surge or a very damp climate? What if there is a fire and your software is destroyed?

7.5

PROTECTING YOUR SYSTEM AND FILES

Obviously, your insurance won't cover all your losses. And there is no way to measure the loss of your databases, your latest book, or all the months of financial records you've been keeping on your computer. Preventing and minimizing loss is an important part of your computerized system. We've already discussed dust, smoke, and static electricity, but keep in mind that electricity and liquids do not mix. Take a break and have that cup of coffee elsewhere. If you buy a fire extinguisher, buy one that contains carbon dioxide or halon, not a liquid.

The most vulnerable parts of your system are its disks, disk drives, and consequently, your files. With a little caution, however, you should never really have a serious problem. If you do have a problem, it is guaranteed that you will never make that mistake again.

Follow these rules when handling your disks:

- Always store your disks in a case that protects them from dust. Keep them in their jackets and NEVER tamper with the permanent covering.
- Never touch the disk itself. Handle it by its cover where the label is located.
- Keep the disk away from heat and moisture and do not bend the disk or otherwise mistreat it.
- Never write on a disk with a pencil or ball-point pen. Write on the label before putting it on the disk. If you must write on the label after it is on the disk, then use a soft, felt-tip pen.

- Keep the disk away from static electricity and magnetic fields. Caution: Your telephone has a magnetic field when it rings. Keep the telephone away from your disks.
- Some computers can damage disks when they are turned off or on. Check your manual. To be on the safe side, remove the disks from the drives before you turn the computer off.
- Buy high-quality diskettes. They will last for years. You don't want to trust your valuable data to an off brand.

You should periodically clean the read/write heads of your disk drives because metallic oxide from the disks can build up on them. All you need is a cleaning kit that looks like one of your disks but is a special fabric with a solvent. You insert the cleaning disk in the drive just like a disk, and it rotates and cleans the heads. If you use your system a lot, you should do this probably once a month.

It is vitally important that you back up your files and practice regular saving procedures. If you leave your computer, even for a few minutes, make a habit of saving whatever you were working on. If you are working on something lengthy, always save it at regular intervals. If anything were to happen, at least you would be assured that most of what you were working on is safely on disk.

Don't fill your disks to capacity; make sure you always have ample room on each disk. Your operating system has a utility that tells you how much room is left as well as how much room a file uses. Delete any unnecessary files from the disk before you start on a big project, or else use a blank disk. To be extra safe when working on a sizable project, regularly save the file to another file, and if it becomes very big, save it to another disk altogether. Just keep thinking: How much can I afford to lose if something should go wrong like a power failure, a defective disk, or running out of room on the disk?

Set up a regular routine of backing up your important files. The end of each working session would probably be the best time. Copy your important files onto another disk and store that disk in another location. It is not impossible for you to put the wrong disk into the wrong drive and ruin your original. Copy your master disk onto a blank disk rather than onto the backup. If anything should go wrong, you at least have the previous generation backup. Old backups can be erased, reformatted, and recycled again. If you transfer files individually, use a different name for your copy file. This minimizes the chance of writing over the original with the copy. Some operating systems transfer files from right to left, others from left to right. If in doubt, write to a new name or a blank disk. Be sure to date the disk backup, especially if you have successive generations of backups. By having successive generations, you are sure to have at least a prior generation backup should something happen to your last. You will still have suffered a loss, but it will not be as great.

How often should you back up a file? That depends on how much you have changed or added to a file, how easy it is to reconstruct a loss, and how much time it would take to recapture the data. You will have to be the judge of that. But keep in mind that even if you have only made a few changes to a file, if you will not be working with that file again for some time, you may easily forget what changes you made. Always keep your backups stored away from the original; if the information is critical, store them preferably at another location. Make two backups and keep one nearby and the second one at the other location. If you don't have a convenient place, then consider getting a safe deposit box.

How about *hard copy* backup? Hard copy is a printout of the computer information. It may seem a little old-fashioned in this electronic age, but I strongly advise it. You can easily become so dependent on a machine that you forget that something can go wrong. But what if something happened to your computer so you could not get to all that electronic data? What if you had to wait several weeks before you could get your computer repaired or replaced? Could you continue doing business? I always make a printed copy of my file, or at least a listing of the most important items in the file, before I make backups. Should something go wrong during the backup procedure, I at least have a hard copy to help me reconstruct the file. I also make copies of invoices, correspondence, and submission documents. I wouldn't want to be in a position of having to write to clients explaining that my computer is in for repairs, and could they please tell me how much they owe me!

As one last precaution, whenever you are finished using a system, always return to the main menu or, even better, the operating system, before shutting the computer off. When a file is written, it is not always written directly to the actual disk but held in a portion of the computer's memory called a *buffer*. Only when the buffer is full does the operating system empty its contents onto the disk. When a program is terminated in its prescribed fashion, the buffer is forced to empty itself into the file. If you terminate the program by shutting off the machine before it has had a chance to go through its termination routine, some of your entries could be lost.

If you are using a hard disk, you might have other problems if you do not back out of a system using the proper procedure. The read/write head has to be returned to a "rest" location. Should you turn off the machine while it is still hovering over your disk, the head will drop and probably damage your disk and data. When you turn your machine on again, you will do even more damage.

7.6

FILES AND DISK ORGANIZATION

Almost all operating systems allow an 8-character file name followed by a dot and a 3-character extension, such as *FILENAME.EXT.* You can assign any name you choose to the first 8 characters and, except for some restrictions, to the 3-character extension. Just to get a feel of what types of file names may be used, list the disk directory of each of the disks containing your software. Your operating system has a command that allows you to do this. First, you may notice some consistency in the way the extensions are used. You may see COM or EXE or command files, BAS for BASIC program files, TXT or MSS for text or manuscript files, BAK for backup files, and so on. To avoid conflict, you should be aware of what extensions are automatically generated by your software before you start assigning file extensions of your own, but you should adhere to convention when required by the software. For instance, your BASIC programs must have an extension of BAS. Your word processing system may also have some rules of its own.

If you start randomly naming files without a system, in no time you will find your disks full of files with names totally meaningless to you. There are several schools of thought on naming files. Some, for instance, frown on using the extension for specific references, so that all your text files should have an extension of TXT and nothing else. Others suggest developing coding schemes so you specifically know what the file is. A coding scheme has merit and may work well for you if you also keep a record of what the file is and what the codes mean.

Keep in mind, though, that in most applications you are going to be working from memory. The directory may not be available to you at the time a program or software is asking you for a file name. I find the simplest solution is to use straightforward, meaningful names that I can remember. However, try to be consistent. As long as there is no conflict, use the extension as a meaningful part of the name. There is no reason why all your letters can't end in .LET, or your invoices in .INV, or your submissions in .SUB. That way you will have little difficulty in tracking down your correspondence with Acme Publishing Company as ACME.LET, ACME.SUB, and ACME.INV. Of course, longer names will require more imaginative abbreviations. Multiple letters might require an ACME2.LET, or you might prefer to make a date part of the name. Just make sure you have a scheme and stick with it.

If you keep a lot of files, you may want to set up a naming system that enables you to delete the files regularly. One of the problems with data processing files is that they can easily be forgotten and stay files forever. Many operating systems allow for purging files on the basis of the extension. For instance, in the CP/M operating system, the command "ERA *.LET" results in the deletion of all files with the extension LET. Now some of those files may be old and some may be new, so you may not want to delete all of them. Instead, consider setting up your extensions for a deletion date. Say you wrote a letter to Acme Publishing in March and decided that you would like to delete that letter from the file in May. You could set up the extension as .L05 where L would indicate it was a letter and 05 the month in which it should be deleted. At the end of May, an "ERA*.L05" would delete all letters you had flagged to be deleted in May, saving you time making separate deletions.

Don't try to keep everything on one disk. They are really not that expensive when you consider the nuisance of having everything crowded together in an illogical manner. Try to reserve each of your data disks for certain types of files. You may have one reserved for your photo files inventory, another for clients, another with correspondence or accounting records. Make sure each disk is clearly labeled and systematically filed in a diskette holder. It is a good idea to print out the directory of each disk as well and keep this list available. Nothing is more annoying than to be in the middle of work and have to return to the operating system because you forgot the spelling of a particular file name.

One helpful approach is to set up your own directory file using your word processor. Enter on the disk the name of each file, a brief description of what the file contains, and maybe a deletion date if it is appropriate. Keep that file on the disk but also print it out so you can refer to it when you are in the middle of a job.

Set aside some time once a month to clean out your disks and get rid of any unwanted files. You will be surprised how fast unnecessary files mount up to clutter your disks. If you start out with an orderly plan and develop good work habits to follow through with that plan, you can avoid chaos later.

7.7

WHAT TO DO WHEN THINGS GO WRONG

It is very unlikely that anything will go wrong with your microprocessor, and in fact most of your hardware will be pretty reliable. When something does go wrong, it may sometimes be a problem with the software, but most often it is something that was done by you, the operator.

Let's say you are going along doing your own thing and suddenly the system halts and doesn't respond to the keyboard, or strange words flash across the screen, or there is a very cryptic message that tells you something is wrong but doesn't give much of a clue as to what it is. Don't panic. Stop. Many people randomly try different keys to get out of the problem, but this could make matters worse. Don't shut the machine off or use the reset button. The worst has probably already happened, so take your time. Even if wild things are flashing across the screen, nothing more is happening than when the machine was sitting there waiting patiently for you to decide to do something. If it is a repeating error message, it will eventually fill the error message buffer and stop. If what is happening on the screen bothers you, put a cover over it.

Now try to remember what you did. If it was something such as inadvertently deleting some data, you can probably recover and continue. If not, pour yourself your favorite beverage, sit back, and pull out your reference manuals. If there was an error message, your manual may give you a better explanation, some ideas of the probable causes, and ways to correct the problem. When you try out the solutions, always keep track of what you do. It could be a bug in the software, and it will help if you can document everything you did before and after the occurrence of the problem in an attempt to correct the situation.

Let's work through a typical problem that you may well encounter someday. You are working with your word processor and are in the middle of a long travel article about your trip to China. You save your file, and suddenly, before the file is completely written, your computer stops, and a message appears, saying, "Disk Write Error," or something even less helpful like "BDOS Error."

First, what should you have done up to this point? You have been saving the file regularly, so you know the problem occurred since you last saved the file. You backed up the file the last time you worked on it, so you know you can salvage at least that much of the article. You checked the room left on the disk before you started, and you thought there was enough. If you didn't do these things, then you have some other problems. But let's say you did do those things. The message can mean two things: either you have encountered a bad track or dirt on the disk, or you have run out of space on the disk.

If you checked the file space and you don't think you could have run out of room, you may have inadvertently signed onto the wrong drive, such as the A drive that has a disk full of software. See if there is a message on your screen that tells you which drive has the problem. If it's the wrong drive, then rewrite the file to a new file name on another drive. If you are on the correct drive and you are sure there is plenty of room, it may be a bad track. Try writing it to a new name on that drive. That may write it to a different place on the disk. If you saved the file recently, you know you were able to write onto the disk at least that far. If you have multiple file capabilities, transfer the next text from the last save and put it into another file. Try writing the file again and then the new piece. If the new piece is small enough, there may be room on your A drive to save it temporarily.

If you did not check your disk drive and you think you are out of room, you will have to make room. If you do not have multiple file capabilities, start deleting text. If you printed some of the article previously or backed it up, then delete the portions you have already saved or printed. Do it a little at a time and then try to write the file. If you are lucky, you may not have overextended your disk capacity too far.

If you do have multiple file capability, consider reducing a file that is no longer needed, or one for which you have a listing or backup and from which you can recapture the data. You can't delete the file, but you can eliminate the data in it, thereby reducing the file size. The whole objective is to minimize your losses and get the file written. Remember, the file must be completely written before you quit the edit function. If it is only partially written, no end-of-file marker would have been written. Without that end-of-file marker, you will not be able to use that file again, and you will lose everything except your last backup. Of course, once you have everything saved, you can transfer what is necessary to other disks using the utilities in your operating system.

7.8

GETTING PERSONAL HELP

You've got this book in your hand, but where else can you get help? Some suggestions already made will be repeated here, so everything will be in one place when you get that sinking feeling in your stomach.

First, there is the computer store where you bought your computer. They will be helpful right after you buy your computer, but it won't take long before the honeymoon is over and their enthusiasm wanes, especially if you haven't bought anything in some time. Sometimes they are just plain busy. They have other customers and new sales to make. If you need help, call or visit when other customers are not likely to be around. Your support really comes from the person who sold you the machine. Other people will help you, although more reluctantly. Unfortunately, the job turnover in computer sales is very high, and the next time you go into the store, your salesperson might not be there. In fact, there may be no one left who remembers you.

Another fact, one you will begin to notice as you become more knowledgeable about computers, is that these people who once awed you with all their technical knowledge don't necessarily know enough to help you in some situations. One reason is that there are just too many things going on in the computer industry for anyone to keep up, much less be an expert. Another reason is that there is such demand for people to staff these computer stores that some of them really aren't that knowledgeable. I know that so far I haven't helped relieve your sinking feeling, and it is probably getting worse.

Many software and hardware distributors maintain 800 (toll-free) "hotline" telephone numbers. They want you to succeed so you will tell everyone what a great product they make. But let's say you are having difficult getting your word processing software to work properly with your printer. The salesman at the computer store has done everything he can but can't get it to work either. So you call up the software people, who tell you that you haven't configured your printer correctly and that you should talk to the vendor who made the printer. You then talk to the printer people, who say they have never heard of your software and have no idea of what information is needed.

Is that sinking feeling getting worse? Actually, if your questions are fairly straightforward, they will try to help you. Many prefer that you document your questions in writing. Put together as much information as possible and, if appropriate, include samples of the problem. They will get back to you.

I think, at this point, it has occurred to you that the only person you can totally rely on is yourself. Unless you are just using the computer for something relatively straightforward, such as word processing or data communications, you are going to have to get a lot smarter about computers.

Subscribe to some of the computer magazines, especially those that specialize in your particular machine. You are not the only one who has had problems, and you will find articles dealing with them. In fact, the magazines may have a very extensive section devoted to answering readers' questions. Read those carefully and don't hesitate to submit your own.

There are probably user groups in your area. These will vary according to interests. Some user groups are technical and cater to hobbyists. You may be confused if you join one of these. Others might specialize in a specific software operating system or in specific computers. These will be a little more along your line of interest. The best user group to join initially is one devoted to your particular machine. Here you will learn all about other people's problems and how they solved them. The more experienced enthusiasts might well be able to help you with your problems. At the very least, join a national group associated with your particular machine. Information on these groups may be included with your computer documentation, or you can ask your salesperson if he or she knows of any user group for your machine. These groups put out a wealth of information in regular newsletters. Not only will these groups help you with your problems, they will also inform you of new products and how they work on your specific system.

Don't overlook friends who also own computers. If they are experienced, they may be willing to spend some time with your problem and help you solve it. People with computers tend to be enthusiastic about sharing knowledge. If they are in the same situation, at least you can cry on each other's shoulders. Actually, just having someone to talk to can help you work through a problem and come to a very obvious solution.

If you are on a network, put out an all-points bulletin on the bulletin board: "Help. Anyone using Ultimatelyperfect Wordwriter with Razzle-dazzle Printer. I need help with the configuration program. Contact XX297." Somebody out there must be able to help you.

Still, the smarter you get, the more you will be able to solve your own problems. Seriously consider taking some classes. Classes are being offered for the more popular software products. Ask your local high school, YMCA, or college if they are offering any computer classes in their adult education programs. Your computer store may also give classes. Sometimes there are special seminars given by consultants or training specialists. Check your computer magazines and the local newspaper to find out if any seminars of this kind are going to be held in your area.

Last of all, keep an eye out for computer trade shows and conferences. Here you may be able to slip in a question to one of the experts at the booth promoting your software or machine. These shows are also a good place to see what is new. Maybe you'll find a better product that is even easier to use, and you can just forget about all of those problems you've been having with your own software.

The ultimate recourse for solving your problems is professional help, but you are going to have to pay for that. However, you may be at a point where you would rather pay someone to handle everything for you.

7.9

GETTING PROFESSIONAL HELP

Why should you seek professional help? For one thing, you may be a very busy photographer. You realize that you could benefit from a computer but don't have the time to do all this work yourself. Or it may be urgent that you get your computer system up and running; you can't wait while you learn all about computers, software, and system design. It is possible that despite all your diligence in learning about computers, you have an application that is just too complex for you, or in spite of all the available software, your application is just too unique and needs custom design and programming.

7.9.1 Types of Data Processing Professionals

When people think of a computer specialist, they think of a programmer. Programmers have high visibility; what they do is tangible. But programming is also very specialized, and it requires a variety of talents to implement computer systems.

Systems analysts are generalists. They have one foot in your business and the other in computer systems. They have to be familiar with both worlds. It is their job to translate your business needs into a computerized system. They evaluate your business needs, design your system, help you with software and hardware selections (if necessary), write up program specifications for a programmer, test the system, put together documentation for you, and assist in your training.

The actual product that an analyst produces is the documentation. Depending on how you use an analyst, you can expect: general specifications outlining how your system is to be implemented on a computer; equipment and software recommendations; detailed program specifications; a plan for testing the program; final user reference manuals on how to specifically use your system. Beware of analysts who don't give you proper documentation. Without documentation, you are totally dependent on them. With documentation, you can discharge an analyst at any stage without suffering any loss.

A programmer translates the specific requirements of an application into machine-readable code. Usually a programmer works from the program specifications written by an analyst. But if you are pretty sure you know specifically what you need, there is no reason why you can't work directly with a programmer. You should, however, write down those instructions so that there is no misunderstanding about what you need and what you finally get from the programmer. The side benefit of writing down the specifications is that you will discover all sorts of things that never occurred to you. Unfortunately, since most people don't realize what a difficult task it is to develop program specifications, they "forget" to include many things or approach the problem in the wrong way. A programmer may turn out the program you requested, but it may not necessarily be the one you wanted, and you may be very unhappy with it.

You should also get some documents and material from the programmer to assure that you are not forever dependent on him or her. In addition, you should get a diskette containing two copies of the program: one of the source code (the human-readable code) and one of the object code (the machine-readable code). You will need the object code to run the program and the source code if you ever want to have the program modified by another programmer. Beware of the programmer who doesn't give you the source code; he is obviously looking for job security. You paid for it, and you are entitled to it. Obtain a listing of the source code and some documentation on how to use it. The programmer should also demonstrate to you that the program performs as you expect and does so without error.

From now on I will be referring to the "data processing consultant." The consultant is most likely an analyst but may also be a programmer. A consultant usually is a specialist in a certain business or in certain types of computer installations. He can advise you or handle any portion of your computerization. If he doesn't have expertise in a certain area, such as programming, he will make sure an adequate programmer is provided and will be responsible for seeing to it that the work is done properly.

7.9.2 Minimizing Cost, Maximizing Use

Consultants are very expensive. Like assignment photographers, they charge by the time it takes to do a job, usually by the day or hour. Occasionally, you can get one to work at a fixed cost, but that is rare, since most people usually don't know what they want initially. You can and should expect an estimate. You have no idea of how much time and money it will take to complete your project. If you have a specific project in mind, the consultant should be able to give you a decent estimate. If you just approach a consultant and say, "I want my business computerized," that becomes a little more difficult. Instead of committing to an entire project, break it down into logical pieces. This way you can control its development and costs and can also find out if you like working with that consultant. After each logical segment is completed, the consultant should be in a good position to estimate the cost of the next segment. If at that point you want to handle the job yourself or find a new consultant, a segment of the job will be totally completed and documented, and you will not have lost money.

Logical breaks in a job for total computer implementation are:

- Reviewing your business and deciding what areas would benefit the most from computerization.
- Reviewing and recommending a computer system and software.
- Designing your computerized system.
- If programming is necessary, writing program specifications; writing the program; testing the program; providing you with user documentation.
- Implementing and installing your system and software.
- Training you in using your system; setting up work procedures; possibly helping you with entering data into the system; providing you with all the documentation you will need to run the system on your own.

Remember, you can have your consultant do all these steps as one project, or you can utilize a consultant for only one or a few steps.

Even within any one project, you can minimize your cost by reducing the time the consultant needs to get the job done. If you have an accountant, you probably keep track of your income and expenses yourself, summarizing them as best you can at the end of the year. You may occasionally ask his advice, but you use him to handle the more complex matters of preparing your taxes that you either do not have time to do yourself or find too complicated. If you just collect all your receipts during the year, dump them in a box, and turn them over to your accountant at the end of the year, you can expect a very big bill for what is essentially simple clerical work which you could have done yourself.

You should do the same for your data processing project. Read through the next chapter to find out what is involved in designing a system. Then have everything ready for your consultant. If necessary, create available work space for the consultant and make yourself available to answer any questions.

7.9.3 Finding and Choosing a Consultant

Actually, the best way to find a consultant is the way you find an accountant, lawyer, or doctor—ask a friend or an associate to recommend one. Most consultants find work on a referral basis. There is one good thing about this system—the consultant has done and probably will do a good job. His next job is dependent on it. Unfortunately, you probably don't know anyone who has used a consultant, or if they have, they may not want to recommend him.

Check with your computer store. They may know of one. What about the salesman at the computer store moonlighting on his own time? He is probably a technical specialist and may be able to handle a programming job for you but is not experienced in developing computer business systems. When it comes to managing your business, find a business specialist. You can also check the Yellow Pages (the "Business-to-Business" book, if your area has one) under "computer" or "data processing consultant."

There are a lot of qualified consultants, but I suspect, because of the explosion of computer interest, there are some people hanging out the consultant shingle who really shouldn't be. Some may overestimate their abilities; they know about computers, they're very enthusiastic about their newfound knowledge, but they are going to be learning the hard realities about business system implementation on *your* nickel.

First of all, your consultant should know business in general. It would be nice if he knew your photography business, but such a specialist would be hard to find. Business knowledge is the key. A computer consultant who works for the aerospace industry will not help you much (unless you want to know the best trajectory for pitching your discarded slides into the wastebasket).

Second, your consultant should know about microcomputers and the software available for them. If all his work has been with IBM mainframes, his perspective and knowledge will be totally unsuitable for your project. But on the other hand, don't think that someone who knows microcomputers will necessarily be the best one for your job. Especially avoid the pitfall of the whiz kid next door, the computer hobbyist, or the person who just got a degree in computer science. They may speak computerese very well and can help you if you have some technical problem using your computer, but they don't have the background to computerize your business.

How can you tell if a consultant is right for you? You can ask for a résumé to find out what sort of background he has. Ask for a client list and contact those clients to find out if they were happy with his work. A personal interview also helps. Follow your own instinct, and don't be intimidated. Does the consultant show a genuine interest and understanding of your business and problems? Does the consultant have some ideas on how those business problems can be solved? Don't expect too much free consulting during an interview, but get some idea of whether the consultant understands your problems and how to solve them. Beware of the consultant that throws around a lot of buzz words and technical terms and doesn't take the time to explain things to you. Chances are he is trying to impress you with his technical knowledge when actually he may not be that competent. Even if he is competent, he is not for you. This is your own personal system, and you are the one who must use it. Part of the consultant's responsibility is to make sure you are comfortable with the system. A consultant who uses a lot of jargon that you do not understand is not trying to make you comfortable; he is trying to make himself indispensable.

There are independent consultants and consulting firms. An independent consultant is just like a freelance photographer—in business for himself. Because he has very little overhead, he is generally less expensive than a consulting firm. When you hire an independent consultant, you know the individual who will be doing the work, and since he is dependent on referrals, he will probably do the best job he can and see your job through to completion. He is more likely to be a specialist. You may even be able to find someone who is familiar with your particular photography business. If he does not have the expertise to do part of the job, he will subcontract to another freelancer who does have that expertise. The main disadvantage to the independent consultant is that there is no backup. If something should happen to your consultant, there is no one to replace him. He may take on too many clients, and since he is only one person, someone may get shortchanged. Also, you have to make the judgment as to whether he is competent to do the job.

The consulting firm has already determined that the individuals they hire are competent. They have a diverse pool of talent on which the individual assigned to your project can call if there is a problem he can't handle. Consulting firms are easier to locate. They may be in the Yellow Pages. They are more likely to be around if you should have problems later. It is possible that the individual assigned to your project may leave the firm, but there are always other people to fill the gap. However, they have executives, offices, advertising, salaries to meet, all of which can add up to a big overhead. Therefore, they will charge higher prices. Also, you don't have control over the individual who will be assigned to your project; that person could be moved from your job to another job. If, however, you really don't like the person assigned to you, most firms will replace him.

8

PLANNING AND DESIGNING YOUR SYSTEM

The secrets to a successful system are organization, ease in maintenance and use, and complete information in a usable form. If you have already purchased a computer, you probably are anxious to get on with it and start making it pay its way. You know what you want, and you already know enough about the software to get it working. Before you dismiss this chapter, heed the following:

- Many systems that are quickly designed and implemented do not work because important information was overlooked, inefficiently presented, or totally wrong for the application. The result: hours of work developing the system and hours, days, or even weeks of putting in data, all wasted. Everything has to be redone. If the second effort is just as sloppy, then it has to be done again. An old data processing saying is "There is never enough time to do the job right the first time but plenty of time to do it again."

- Many systems that are not adequately tested will fail and cause disastrous results. It is so easy to start trusting a computerized system—after all, you know computers never make mistakes. But humans often do, and occasionally even a machine fails. Let's say you have your system up and running, you've coded in all two thousand of your clients, and then, mysteriously, clients start to disappear, or wrong data appear in their records, or when you select clients on the basis of some criterion, the selection was not what you expected. The first problem is that you will not notice these things immediately; the second is that you will not know the extent of the problem. How many times did you send the same letter to the same client? Or what client didn't get any letter at all? And, finally, how are you going to recover from this? When a computer system goes wrong, either it does it in insidious ways that are difficult to identify and correct, or it does it in massive ways, leaving you with a huge clerical job.

- Failure to provide adequate backup or alternative systems can have a devastating effect on your business. Many businesses have ceased to exist because they became totally dependent on their new computer system and did not do the proper planning, designing, and testing or provide for recovery in case of failure.

Don't let all this discourage you. These potential disasters can be eliminated, or at least minimized, if care is taken in the design and implementation of your system. Follow the suggestions in this chapter and don't jump into the project without some thoughtful planning.

8.1

DECIDING WHAT TO DO

First, you have to do some housekeeping. It is hard to make order out of chaos. Catch up on all that filing. Put away everything into whatever filing systems you have now. That includes both your photo files and your business files. Bring everything up to date. If you have been meaning to update all those index cards, do it now.

There are several reasons for going through these housekeeping chores. The first is that it will be easier for you to plan your new systems if your old systems are in order. Second, in order to put your new systems in operation, you have to collect all your old data and input it into the new system. With all the drudgery out of the way, you are ready to start fresh. And finally, if you intend to continue doing business while you are implementing your new system, you will need to continue working off the old system until your new one has been tested.

Now, with a pad of paper, start writing down the types of things you are doing now, the types of files you are maintaining, the types of forms or correspondence you have, and even some of the things you would like to do but never have been able to do. Consult Chapter 4, Getting Down to Business, for some ideas. At this point, don't try to make any choices. Just jot down your ideas.

You can't do everything at once, so you will now have to set some priorities and order your list in terms of those priorities. This may be very easy or very difficult. For instance, if you purchased the computer to help you with your writing, you will want to start learning word processing. This is a good choice, because you deal with just one type of software first, in a straightforward, simple application. If you did not want the computer for a single-minded purpose, your choices will be more complex. Consider some of the following in your decision:

- *Learning your software:* This can be dull if you don't have something meaningful to do. But you don't necessarily want to put a great deal of work into developing a complex but unworkable client file just to learn your way around the software capabilities. Why not start with an unimportant application that will help with learning but won't risk hours of effort and serious failure if it doesn't work right? For instance, put all the names and addresses of your friends into your file management system. Then try writing a form letter, using your word processing system, telling your friends about your new computer. Now run the form letters against your address file. This is good practice for the real thing, and failure to get it going won't have dire consequences. Besides, you probably haven't written to your friends in years.
- *Ease of implementation:* This is sometimes the best reason for putting in a system. Psychologically, if nothing else, it is a great boost to your enthusiasm. You really have something up and running on your computer, it wasn't difficult, and it took very little time. If you have an application that fits into this category, I strongly recommend that you make it your first. How do you know it is something easy? Ask yourself a few questions. Is the software you must use simple for you to learn? Are there just a few types of data needed to make the system work? Is it a standalone application that need not work with another system?
- *Volume of work:* Remember that the computer helps the most with repetitive tasks and those using large number of items. If you find yourself swamped with work on a certain task, that task might be a good candidate for your first computer application. For instance, you want to mass-mail your brochure to hundreds of potential clients you found in *Photographer's Market.* You could set up a simple mailing address file using your file management system and print address labels using your mail generator. The only caution is: Do not take on as your first attempt an

application that is too complex. You do not want to become discouraged with your first effort.

- *Immediacy of work:* Some things you do have to accomplish right away, whether they are to be done manually or on the computer. Consider this category for first selection only if the task is simple and is not so immediate that you would have no time to do the job by hand. For instance, you may have a form letter you want to send to several clients. This is a reasonable choice as long as you leave yourself enough time to photocopy the letter, plus type in all the names and addresses, should your attempts at starting up your computer system fall short of expectations. If it is April 14 and you must get your taxes done, do them by hand.
- *Interrelationship of applications:* This would not be considered in your choice of which system to try first but in how to set up subsequent priorities. The implementation of one system may affect the design of another, so you will want to place them together or at least close to each other when determining your priorities. This may include setting up query letters with your word processing system, which will be interfaced with a client file developed by using your file management system.

Now return to your list of tasks, ranking them according to the above criteria. Put them in the order that you want to do them. Remember, for your own motivation, make sure the first application is easy and that you plan to implement your system one step at a time.

A schedule is necessary to help you organize your efforts and to give you some idea of when you will get each task done. If tax time is six months away, this may seem to be plenty of time, until you see by the schedule that prior projects may take eight months. Thus you may want to change your priorities. Your schedule depends on the initial number of tasks you want to do (don't try to schedule everything), the amount of time you can spare to work on your new systems (you may have other work to do), and the complexity of software use and system implementation. Estimate the number of hours or days it will take to do each job, allowing time to learn the software. Multiply those estimates by three and record the start and completion dates based on those numbers. Why three? The number three is quite arbitrary but it is closer to the actual time it will take than the estimate you made. No matter how seasoned people may be in implementing computer systems, they are always optimistic whenever they start out with a new one. But everything will take longer than expected, and more things will go wrong than anyone could have imagined.

8.2

DESIGNING YOUR INFORMATIONAL NEEDS

While you are trying to make up your mind about which application to do first, start collecting samples of everything that might relate to your computer system. The data processing term for this is *data gathering.* Gather every form letter, price list, stock list, agreement form—anything you regularly or even infrequently send out to clients. Also get samples of any index files or control forms you maintain. If your index files are free form, take an index card and write out the information you *should* have on a complete card. Since some information may only exist in physical form, such as your photo files, you should try to summarize on paper your filing scheme.

Don't put down your pencil yet. Write down the tasks involved in your typical activities. For instance: you have sent a query and your stock list to a client who writes back to say he wants some pictures. What tasks do you have to do?

1. Locate and pull the pictures requested.
2. Log out pictures pulled.
3. Prepare a letter indicating that you are submitting pictures per his request.
4. Prepare submission terms.
5. Type up numbers and descriptions of pictures being sent.
6. Set up file folder for client.
7. Mark on the index card the date the pictures were sent.
8. Package pictures, type client and return address labels.

Your list may not look exactly like this, but the idea is to determine all the steps taken to send out those pictures. This "work-flow procedure" will give you a better idea of the relationships of tasks. The subject will be covered in more detail in the section on "Work flow."

Now that you have all your samples and procedures, it is time to get down to work.

8.2.1 Setting Up Form Letters

Let's say you want to implement a system where you can select information from a client file to insert into personalized form letters. First, pull out all your form letters. Each of these will be put into separate computer files, using your word processing system. You will be using your mail generator system to combine information from your client and letter files into a personalized letter. If you have not worked with this software yet, take the time to review the documentation. Are there any restrictions or limitations on the form letters? Must they adhere to a specific form? How are insertions indicated to the mail generator?

Now take your letters and mark, with brightly colored ink, those areas of the letter with variable information (name and address, salutation, and date). If you want to improve the letter, this is the time to do it. Note some of the nice extras your software might give you to make a more personal letter. For instance, you may be able to vary a particular paragraph in a given letter; you might want to use one paragraph in a letter to a book publisher and another in a letter to a magazine editor. Your software probably allows you to indicate which paragraph should

---

FILE: STOCK.LET

(DATE)

(CONTACT)
(TITLE)
(COMPANY)
(STREET ADDRESS)
(CITY), (STATE) (ZIP)

DEAR (SALUTATION),

I AM A TRAVEL PHOTOGRAPHER AND HAVE OVER TEN THOUSAND PHOTOGRAPHS OF POINTS OF INTEREST IN THE UNITED STATES, EUROPE, ASIA AND AFRICA. JUST RECENTLY, I RETURNED FROM A TRIP TO MAINLAND CHINA AND HAVE SEVERAL HUNDRED PICTURES OF THE TOURIST ATTRACTIONS IN THAT COUNTRY. I HAVE ENCLOSED MY STOCK LIST. MAY I SEND YOU A SELECTION OF PICTURES? ENCLOSED IS A CONVENIENT POSTCARD FOR YOUR REPLY.

I AM LOOKING FORWARD TO DOING BUSINESS WITH (NAME OF COMPANY).

SINCERELY,

8-A. A Sample Form Letter

---

be used for each type of letter. The software may also allow insertions, which can be automatically pulled from the client file. These add a more personal touch to your machine-produced letters. For example, you can end your letter with "I am looking forward to doing business with ACME Publishing Company." The "ACME Publishing Company" was, of course, automatically inserted by your computer. Mark areas for personalized touches but don't overdo it.

Work out a file-naming scheme for your letters, assign a file name to each letter, and write it on the top of the sample letter. These will all be filed in a notebook so you can select the letter you need and identify it by its file name. When you are finished, you can put the letter on the appropriate disk using your word processing system.

8.2.2 Designing Reports

There may be times when you will want printed listings of information from your files. For instance, you might want an alphabetical listing of all clients with their addresses, a listing of paper-product clients, or a listing of clients with outstanding balances (including the balance amounts). Your file management system probably has a built-in report generator to do this for you. Before you get too deep into designing your reports, you may want to review the documentation that came with the report generator for any rules or restrictions. If you are going to have the report custom programmed, you will still be following these design procedures.

The width of your report is limited by the capabilities of your printer. You must find out the maximum number of characters your printer can print across. The printer will use paper 8½ inches wide, the width of normal typing paper. If your printer prints 10 characters to the inch, that totals 85 characters; at 12 per inch, it will be 102.

You may have purchased a printer that prints on wide computer paper. This is great if you want your reports to show a great deal of information. Typical computer paper allows 132 characters on a ten-to-the-inch printer and 158 characters on a twelve-to-the-inch. Normal page length will give you 66 lines on your six-line-to-the-inch printer and 110 lines on your ten-line-to the inch printer.

It is easier to design a report if you have a special form that shows the lines and character spacing. These forms may be called "report layout forms" or "printer spacing charts." They are usually only available through computer form distributors servicing larger businesses. If you plan on designing many reports, you might try to obtain some of these forms. Be sure to get one that fits the line and spacing requirements of your printer.

If you are printing a report on paper only 8½ inches wide, you may prefer to use the word processor for design work. The cursor can mark off the character positions. Just remember to turn off the automatic fill so you can use all eighty columns. Actually, there are some report generators that allow you to draw right on the screen, but even with these you may prefer the word processor for initial planning.

Now it is time to be creative. Write down the names of the information you want to print and the greatest number of characters that can be contained in your file for that item. Using your special form or word processor, mark an "X" in each column or print space for the maximum number of characters for each type of information to be printed. If you run out of room, you will either have to eliminate some items from this report, or if your report generator allows it, print a second line. In most cases, it is better to print another report than a second line. The only exception would be if the second line contained related information: for instance, client address lines following client name line, or a multiline list of photos sent to client.

Once everything fits, space it out neatly with adequate space between each item. At this point, think of a name for each item. These names will be printed as a heading above the item and must fit in the same number of characters. You will either have to be clever with abbreviations or adjust the spacing between data items to accommodate the

BILLING SUMMARY
SEPTEMBER 99, 1999

PAGE ______

CLT NO	CLIENT NAME	INV DATE	TYPE	NO PICS	AMT DUE
______	______	MM/DD/YY	___	99,999	99,999.99
______	______	MM/DD/YY	___	99,999	99,999.99
______	______	MM/DD/YY	___	99,999	99,999.99
______	______	MM/DD/YY	___	99,999	99,999.99
______	______	MM/DD/YY	___	99,999	99,999.99
______	______	MM/DD/YY	___	99,999	99,999.99
______	______	MM/DD/YY	___	99,999	99,999.99
______	______	MM/DD/YY	___	99,999	99,999.99
______	______	MM/DD/YY	___	99,999	99,999.99
______	______	MM/DD/YY	___	99,999	99,999.99
______	______	MM/DD/YY	___	99,999	99,999.99
______	______	MM/DD/YY	___	99,999	99,999.99
		TOTAL		999,999	999,999.99

8-B. Sample Report

headings. This will usually be the case with one-character codes.

Now, in case you are turning this project over to a programmer, it is customary to show the alphabetic data as *X*, the numeric data as *9*, and items such as dates as *MM/DD/YY.* Make sure your marks represent the largest length of data possible, and include all punctuation you want to see. It is easier to read a report if your alphabetic data is left-adjusted to line up with your heading, your numeric data is right-adjusted to line up with your heading, and your codes are centered.

Now that you have the body of your report designed, it is time to do the headings. Put in your title, subtitle, and page number, spacing it the way you will want to see it on the final report. Titles and subtitles are usually centered or left-adjusted. Page numbers are normally put on the upper right-hand corner of the report. Finally, indicate any line spaces and totals. If you are not using a specially designed printer form, you may want to mark in the left-hand margin the line number where you want the item to appear. You might want to mark the character spacing every five spaces so you don't have to keep counting. Your report generator or programmer will need to know the column and possibly the line location of each item. If you are using a report generator, you might want to write down the *tag names* (covered in the section on file design) of each data item. Now when you sit down at your computer with your report generator, you will have all the information right in front of you.

8.2.3 Designing Files

A computer keeps data in files. These are quite similar to the manual files where you now keep information. Within the files are records, which are complete sets of information (such as all information on a particular client). Within each record there are fields that are specific items of information. We will be assuming that you are working with a file management system rather than a database system. In fact, I recommend that you start with a file management system. A database system will require more training and much more time to work out data relationships.

As with designing reports, it is better if you sit down to do some planning before attempting to use the software. You can design a file for any sort of information you want to keep or retrieve, but let's work with the client file as an example. Get your sample index card and any files you now keep. If these are valuable, you will want to build on them.

Make a list of all the information you keep on a client. If the item is a code, even a color code, record what each code means. A *code* is a value used to group data with similar characteristics. For instance, magazine publishers could be coded as *M* or book publishers as *B*. Include all information, even if you keep that information in a supplementary file. List any additional information that you would like to keep about a client but haven't been. Try to make your list as complete as possible, since it could be difficult to add information to the file later.

Go through your list and put down the number of characters necessary to describe each item. If you want to be able to group some clients together, such as book publishers or poster companies, assign a code instead of a description. If you want to send something out to just your book publishers and you have identified them with a code *B*, then it is an easy matter for your computer to select all records with that code.

It is not necessary to make something a code if a description is better. Sometimes the presence or absence of data can act as a code; for example, presence of the billing date indicates that a bill was sent. In some cases, you might want to keep some data in a supplementary file; for instance, a list of all the pictures you sent to the client. You should indicate the record identification of that supplementary information on your master file so you can locate it.

After you have a complete list of data items, you must decide which one of those data items is to be used to uniquely identify the record. This is usually referred to as the *key*. The key is what you use to locate and file the record and could be such things as the client's name or a number assigned to the client. You probably kept your files and index cards in some sort of order so that you could locate an individual client.

The computer also must be able to locate an individual client, although it probably will not physically keep the records in any order. Check back with your software documentation. There may be some restrictions on what you can use for a key, such as key size. You have to live with its rules. Some systems may allow multiple keys, which allow you to locate a record on the basis of two or more criteria. (You may want to locate a client by both name and number.) Some software may only allow one key, and it has to be the first field on the record. Some may limit you to a number or may even assign the number. Note how your system works so you can plan your record to work on your software.

Let's assume your software is flexible enough to allow the use of any type of data for a key. If you keep your files alphabetically, you may want to continue to use this method. There are two things to consider when using a name as a key in a computerized system. One is that you must enter it on the record in the precise form that you'll use to retrieve it. If your file consists of business names only, you will not have serious problems, but if it contains personal names, you will have to be very careful how you set up your name fields. Let's say you have John Smith as a client. John Smith is recorded on an index card and is filed alphabetically under "Smith." You know where the last name is, but a computer doesn't. You must either make the field "Smith, John" or two fields

"John" and "Smith," where the last name field "Smith" is the key.

The second problem is that computers expect exact data—close is not enough. So if you put in "Smith John," "Smith, John T." or "Smith Jr., John," but your record contains "Smith, John," you are not going to find your record. Every character must be exactly the same as it is on the record, including spaces and punctuation. Some file management software will allow you to search through similar records until you find the one you recognize. For example, you might be able to just put in "Smith" and have the system page through every "Smith" record until you see the one you want. Check your documentation to see if it allows this.

Computers work better when each record is identified as a number (though it need not be strictly numeric). That is why you have so many numbers (social security, checking account, telephone, credit card, and so on). Even if you want to use an alphabetical key, you may also want to use a number for quick, unique identification. Of course, your software must support multiple keys. Some software will only let you use numbers. This will be a major problem with files that require name identification, such as the one you will design to locate your photos by subject. For our sample client file, however, this would not be a problem, since a client number lends itself to this type of file. Just be sure there is a master list of client numbers and names, and try to include the client number on all correspondence. (Your report generator can give you an alphabetical list of your clients and their numbers.)

Your file management program probably does some editing; that is, it will check certain data elements to make sure they are correct when you enter them into the system. Look in your file management documentation to find out what your software checks. At a minimum it will probably check if the data is alphabetical or numeric, and field size. Go through the list and identify each item as purely alphabetical data, purely numerical data, or a combination of the two. If your system checks for valid codes or number ranges, put those down where appropriate. A valid code would be something like "A" for Active and "I" for Inactive. A number range might be 01-99 for number of days a client can hold pictures. Some systems allow you to require that data be entered into a field, or will copy data from another record, or will enter a default value if nothing is entered. These options help insure the accuracy of your data and will speed up your data entry.

The last thing you need to do is write down a tag or data name. (Your software may call it by a different name or will assign the name if the software does the formatting.) Your data element will actually have two names: one that appears on the screen to prompt you but has no meaning to the program, such as CLIENT NAME; and one that is used internally by the program to identify that piece of data you call CLIENT NAME. You may assign that data name, but your software may have some rules you must follow, such as the maximum number of characters you may use. Some valid data names for your client name might be "client," "cname," or "client.name." Make up a data name for each data element.

CLIENT MASTER FILE
DATA LIST

PROMPT	LENGTH	TYPE	DATA NAME	EDIT RULES
*CLIENT NO	5	AN	CLIENT.NO	REQUIRED
*CLIENT NAME	30	AN	CLIENT.NAME	REQUIRED
ADDRESS-1	30	AN	CLIENT.ADD1	REQUIRED
ADDRESS-2	30	AN	CLIENT.ADD2	
CITY	20	AN	CLIENT.CITY	REQUIRED
STATE	2	A	CLIENT.STATE	VALIDATE AGAINST STATE TABLE
ZIP	5	N	CLIENT.ZIP	REQUIRED
CONTACT	25	AN	CONTACT	
SALUTATION	25	AN	SALUTATION	REQUIRED
TITLE	25	AN	TITLE	
TELEPHONE	10	N	TELEPHONE	
DATE PICTURES SENT	6	N	SENT.DATE	FORMAT MM/DD/YY
NO PICTURES SENT	5	N	SENT.NO	
PIC LIST NO	4	N	SENT.LIST	
DATE BILLED	6	N	BILL.DATE	FORMAT MM/DD/YY
AMT BILLED	7	N	BILL.AMT	FORMAT 99999.99
INVOICE NO	4	N	BILL.INV	
STATUS	1	A	STATUS	MUST BE A OR I; DEFAULT A
CLIENT TYPE	1	A	TYPE	MUST BE B, M OR C
DATE ENTERED	6	N	ENT.DATE	SYSTEM DATE

CLIENT MASTER FILE

CLIENT NO _____

CLIENT NAME ______________________________
ADDRESS-1 ______________________________
ADDRESS-2 ______________________________
CITY ______________________ STATE ___ ZIP _____

CONTACT ____________________________ SALUTATION ____________________________
TITLE ____________________________

TELEPHONE ___-___-___

DATE PICTURES SENT ___/___/___ NO PICTURES SENT ______ PIC LIST NO ______
DATE BILLED ___/___/___ AMT BILLED ______ INVOICE NO ______

STATUS (A=ACT,I=INACT) ___ CLIENT TYPE (B=BOOK,M=MAG,C=CAL) ___

DATE ENTERED ___/___/___

8-C. Data List and Screen Layout

Now it is time to design your screen. Some systems are very rigid in their rules for screen design; others will design the screen for you. Most will let you design your own.

Your word processor is a great tool for designing screens. Bring up a new file using your word processor and turn off the "fill mode." Input a title identifying the file on the top of the blank screen. It is always good practice to put a title on each screen so that many months from now, when you have numerous files, you will know which file you are using. Use all capital letters for prompts so that your data stand out from the prompts. Your software may even go one step further and highlight your prompts by using reverse video or by making the prompts brighter. The prompts should be kept short but meaningful. They are for your benefit, so if you have difficulty remembering a code, put it in the prompts. For example, CLIENT STATUS (A-ACTIVE, I-INACTIVE). Note, though, that some file management systems may restrict the size and form of the prompt. Check your documentation. The actual space where you will be entering the data will be marked with dashes, with one dash for each character allowed.

The order in which you put the data is mainly up to you, depending on how you want the screen to look. Generally, the key will be the first data item. Some systems may require that it be the first item. Related items are best grouped together, such as name and address or information related to billing. Items that are changed or referenced most frequently should be put toward the top of the screen; those less frequently, at the bottom.

Names are very important but can cause some difficulty. First, always make sure your name field is big enough. If you run out of room in the address field, you can always abbreviate it, but people don't take too kindly to having their names abbreviated. If you are not using a name as part of a key, it would be better to put the name in one field, first name followed by last name. If there is a possibility that you may have to reference just the last name, then make it two fields. Do check with your software documentation to be certain you can get the two name fields back together. If not, you may need one field for the full name and one for just the last name. If you'll be using your file for letter writing, set up a separate field for the salutation. A computer can only follow specific rules. If you decide that you will be always using the last name in your salutation, your computer won't know if the proper address should be Mr., Ms., or Dr. Some people you might prefer to greet by their first name or even a nickname. You will want to make your salutation exactly the way you want it on the letter: e.g., Mr. Smith, Dr. Jones, Jack, Aunt Millie.

Once you have designed a screen you like, then print it out. With the data list and screen format design in front of you, you can create your file using the file management system.

8.3

TESTING

Now that you have spent so much time learning about computers, purchasing the equipment and software, evaluating and organizing your business, and finally designing exactly what you need, you're probably tired of all this and want to get the system going. *Don't.* Test the system first. Even though testing is tedious, if you bypass it now, you are going to regret it. You certainly wouldn't buy a new camera and use it on an important assignment without testing it; you would run a roll of film through it first. You should follow this same wise procedure with your computer systems.

Testing is intended to accomplish several things. It is, of course, supposed to find all the errors in the system. You are also testing the design of the system. You may find you've designed a client file that has inadequate field sizes or that misses some important fields.

Test the integrity of the system. One system may not work with another system the way you thought it would. For instance, my first file management system came with a name and address template. I tested it with my mail generator to see how well it produced form letters. It worked very well. However, I did not like the way the template was designed, so I set up my own name and address fields. When I tested my new file, it didn't work the way I wanted. When it printed the names, titles, and addresses, it left blank lines where I had omitted titles or second address lines. It was totally unsatisfactory, so I had to go back and use the system's template. If I hadn't tested it, I would have wasted my time keying in all those names and addresses.

The last thing to test is ease of use. You may set up a system that seems perfect, but in actual practice it is really too difficult to use and must be abandoned for a different system.

A professional consultant will actually write down a test plan. Each step of the plan will have a certain test objective, containing the test data he will use and the expected results. It would be a good idea if you wrote down a test plan as well.

Your first step will be *unit testing:* i.e., testing the simple functions of the system. You will want to test for the following in a file management system:

- Valid Data: Put correct data in each field and see if it is accepted. Write the record and test the retrieval; see that it works and that all the data are there. Change the data in all fields. Try all valid codes to test for their acceptance. Input invalid codes into every field to see if they are rejected; use different types of codes such as numeric and alphanumeric.

- Fields and Field Sizes: Put in some typical data from a dozen randomly selected index cards. It is easy to underestimate the size of fields. Try to find some examples of long fields and cards with a great deal of information.
- Error Conditions: Introduce error conditions to see how the system handles and recovers from them. Test not only your record but all the operations you have to use, such as writing and retrieving the record. Put in strange keys and see what happens.
- Relational Changes: Sometimes a change to one field should result in the system changing another field. Test all of these to make sure they do in fact function in the way you expect. Make these tests simple, doing only one type of change at a time. Sometimes other fields might change, so you will want to monitor the procedure carefully to see what is happening.
- Garbage: In data processing terms, bad data are called "garbage." Garbage causes systems to do strange things. You know what your system will do, so you will, without realizing it, test your system in a very narrow way. But someday you will accidentally hit a key that causes strange things to happen. So for this test, a monkey or, lacking that, a three-year-old child is handy. If one or the other is not available, have someone who is unfamiliar with your system try to cause some havoc.

Once you are sure the pieces of the system work fine individually, do some *system testing;* i.e., test them as they should work together. In the unit test, you developed a test file that had good data and bad data in it. First, run that file through all the other systems to see what happens. These systems will include report writing, special forms, interfacing with your word processing form letters, and so on.

After you are sure that these other systems will survive, you must build a test file that is representative of the types of functions you will be doing with your system. For instance, you may want to send your query letter to selected groups in the database. You will be selecting records on the basis of information in some field. Maybe you want to send your stock list to book publishers only. Put in some book publishers and some non-book publishers and then select only book publishers. There also may be times when you might want to select clients on the basis of several conditions. For instance, you may want to go through your file of wedding clients one year after their weddings to send them an anniversary letter reminding them that you do family portraits. In this case you will be selecting wedding clients and their wedding dates plus one year.

Unit testing results are easy to evaluate; system testing is a bit more involved. This is why professionals use written test plans. You are trying to determine if your systems are receiving all the data they should and are processing it in the way you expect. For instance, if you are selecting new clients who never received your stock list, you will be selecting them on the basis of the date the record was put in the system. In your test file you would then set up records having dates before and after the cutoff date and some that are actually on the cutoff date. Go through your file and write down the records you expect as a result of your test. When you run the test, compare your predictions with the results. Specifically check to see if anyone was included who shouldn't have been or was missed when he should have been included.

You will now want to test how your computer system works with your everyday business procedures. When you put information into your computer system, you will probably be working from some sort of document, such as a postcard response to a query. You will want to see how conveniently organized that source information is. Do you have to use several documents? Is the order of information on the documents different from the order of input in the computer system? You should have taken these things into consideration when you first designed the system, but this is where you test it out. Use some actual business situations and try them out from beginning to end.

The final test is a *parallel test;* that is, you maintain and run the new and old systems simultaneously. Let me explain why you should do this, and then let me suggest some alternatives. No matter how diligently you have tested a system, there are always some gremlins in there just waiting to wreak havoc. That is why you didn't want to be the first person to use a new piece of software. But now this is your software, and you are the only one who will shake the "bugs" out.

Let's say you have a system that keeps track of who has your pictures, how much money they owe you, and when they paid you. You have been handling this information adequately on index cards. But now you have a computer system. You've tested it, and it works perfectly. So you begin using the computer, and you stop using your index cards. You add several new clients to your file, send out many pictures, and make lots of sales. Everything is going great, but after a month or so you get a nagging feeling that something is wrong, but you can't figure out what. Then you go to update a particular client and find that his record is gone. After some very lengthy detective work, you discover that on the thirteenth day of the month, the system deletes an arbitrary number of records. They're gone, and you don't even know which ones they were. There may be clients in that group who owe you money or have your pictures. You don't know who they are, and you can't go back to your index cards because they're out of date.

A parallel test enables you to discover this problem sooner and gives you an alternative system when the computer system fails. During a parallel test, you regularly compare the output of one system against that of the other and note any differences. How long should you parallel? That depends on the system and how disastrous a failure might be. You should run it through all change cycles. For instance, an accounting system has some month-end and year-end processing that would be different from its everyday processing. But when it's only January, you don't look forward to maintaining two systems for a whole year. What you can do is force a year-end test on both systems. Run them for a couple of months, and when you are satisfied that they work, do a year-end closing. (Be sure to make a copy of your live system and run the copy as the test.) Have your computer system do all its year-end closing and produce all its year-end reports. Meanwhile, you sit down with your calculator and do all the totaling for your manual system. Compare the results. If everything looks good, then you can make a decision to continue with your computer system alone.

Now for the good news. You *should* parallel, but you probably won't want to do it. Only you can decide how serious a computer problem would be to your business situation. The problems vary according to the type of application with which you are dealing. An alternative to a full-blown parallel test is a *pilot implementation*. You take a sample of your business and computerize it while still continuing your manual system. Maybe you decide to put magazine clients on your computerized system. There are enough to test the system, but not so many that you find the job overwhelming. If it works for magazine clients, then it will probably work for book publishers and your paper-product clients.

8.4

WORK-FLOW PROCEDURES

Pull out all those procedures you wrote down when you were data gathering. Some of these will stay the same; some will require additional steps that now include your computer systems; some will have to be completely rewritten. The way you will be doing business now is quite different from the way you did business before.

For instance, when you sent out query letters, you probably did a few a day or a few a week. It was a boring and time-consuming job. Your stock list was probably constantly out-of-date. Your old procedure might have read:

1. Make a list of prospective clients from reference books.

2. Type query letter.

3. Type envelope.
4. Type client name and address on return postcard.
5. Pull stock list from file.
6. Stuff the envelope.

Then you went on to type the next query letter.

You won't do it that way with your computer system, but rather like this:

1. Update your stock list. (That is now easy since you can change it but don't have to retype it.)
2. Get names and addresses of some prospective clients from a reference book. These you will now input to your client file.
3. Print all the letters, envelopes, name and address labels, postcards, and copies of your stock list.

All this paper spills out of the printer, but you now have to think about combining it properly and efficiently. Since everything comes out in the same order, you might want to set up a table as a staging area with your stacks of letters, envelopes, postcards, labels, and stock lists arranged for ease of quick packaging and mailing.

Take some time to think about each operation and the most efficient way to handle it. A small change in your manual or computer system could make a big difference. Write out these new procedures; this is a good way to walk it through.

Your work-flow procedures should also include the new housekeeping chores related to the computer. Housekeeping is exactly that—it includes cleaning up files on the disks, doing backups, putting your files in order, and checking your controls. These all should be done regularly as part of your business routine.

8.5

PLANNING FOR COMPUTER FAILURE

You may never have a computer problem. The computer is actually quite reliable in spite of the occasional gremlin. The problem is that when something does go wrong, it is often difficult to discover and then correct the error. Don't forget: These machines are unthinking idiots. That is why you have to plan for computer failure. It's like insurance: You insure your camera, your car, your house, and even your computer. You may never need that insurance, but if something does happen, you'll be very glad you have it. There are actually two types of procedures to consider: *monitoring* and *recovery.*

In a previous example, gremlins suddenly decided on the thirteenth day of the month to drop several client records. The problem is that since the computer file has many records, you will not notice that some are missing, especially since you cannot physically "see" the records. The simple solution is to *count the records.* Computers count very well and very fast. When you are finished with your client additions, ask the computer for a record count. The computer count from the last time you added clients, plus the number of new records you added, should add up to today's count. If they do not, it is probably your fault, so check that first before you fire the computer. You may have missed a client or put the same one in twice.

But if everything is accounted for and the difference is monumental, you can suspect the computer system. What you can do about it will be covered a little later. So design these count checks into your system as much as possible and have them tie back to some counts in another system or to your own manual counts.

Dollar amounts should also be monitored. The computer doesn't recognize the "reasonableness" of amounts the way you do. If you erroneously entered fifty thousand dollars instead of five thousand dollars, you would probably notice it. But if it were part of the hundred or so jobs you did that month for fifty dollars and one went in as five dollars, would you notice? You should batch all these types of transactions together and add them up yourself, and then have the computer give you a total of all your input for a comparison of the two totals. You should also have ways of balancing amounts as they are passed from file to file to make sure nothing is "lost." For instance, after your accounting system does its monthly processing, does the total of the daily input equal the monthly total?

These checks will help you catch problems, but what about recovery, especially if you do not discover a problem right away? We talked about backups as a way of salvaging a lost file if something should happen while you were working on it. But what if you have been dutifully backing up your current file each day, only to find that the problem has been going on for weeks and you don't have the data anywhere anymore? You have to think in terms of the types of disasters that might happen, the degree of difficulty in reconstructing the file, the critical importance of the systems to everyday business activities, and the alternative solutions available to you. Let's start with the simple and move up to the more complex problems so you can maintain your perspective.

What if your roof leaks, soaking the diskette containing your form letters? What if the backup disk was sitting right beside it and also got soaked? This may not be too critical. Your backup in this case would also be hard copy as well as the backup disk that should have been stored elsewhere. You'll have extra work putting everything back on disks, but maybe you'll need only a few of those form letters immediately.

If the file is critical and would take a long time to recover, make two backup disks, keeping one at another location along with a hard copy. Say you are working on a book when a fire breaks out, destroying your disks and machine. How would you recover? You may still have the hard copy, though it may need to be retyped. You also should have the backup disk at another location, plus you could rent machine time to finish the job.

Problems can accumulate in a file for which immediate backup would not help. Master files, like your client file, fall into this category. For this, you will periodically need hard copy backup of your file plus some sort of hard copy record of what was done since the last hard copy listing.

You will also want to keep generation backups. Let's say you input new data into your system every day, and each day you print out the input for that day. Once a week you print out the whole file to spot-check it for errors. In this case you will want to keep a copy of the file when you last printed it as well as the current backup. If something went wrong during that period, you have a record of everything you did and would only have to reinput all the changes from that last period. The number of backup generations you keep and the time between those generations depends on the frequency of your changes and your recovery procedure. Diskettes are relatively cheap. You could make a separate backup of the file every day for a full month if you think it is worth it. If you find that a problem occurred five days ago, then you only have to go back five days to recover your data. Make sure you do keep backups of major changes to your files. Your accounting system will do some major updating at month's end and year's end. You may want to keep several generations of month-end files as well as daily backups.

Don't overlook manual recovery systems. If your computer broke down for a month or so, what would you do? Although it would be inefficient, you should be sure that you can always go back to some sort of manual system for the more critical tasks. In short, don't get rid of your typewriter, and always keep hard copy files.

9

USING YOUR SOFTWARE

It's impossible to tell you how to use every type of software package available on the market today. That would take an encyclopedia! This chapter will give you some advice and guidelines on ways to approach and use some of the most important software functions. Beyond that you are at the mercy of the documentation that came with your software.

This chapter will also help you implement some of the software into your unique working environment. You can use the software and documentation just as it comes out of the package, but you may want to customize it for your use.

9.1

LEARNING TO USE SOFTWARE

Although you are impatient to get started with your system, allow yourself time to learn how to use it. Learning to use a computer is as simple as learning to use a light switch; learning to use the software is another matter.

Don't try to learn everything in one day. Set aside a certain time every day to concentrate on learning your system. Accept the fact that you will make mistakes. Be patient with yourself; the machine will be infinitely patient with you. Follow these rules:

1. Don't try to learn all your different software packages or functions at once. Not only is it a big task, but you will become confused. Even if the two packages claim to use similar instruc-

tions, there will be just enough difference to confuse you when switching from one to the other. Pick one function and stick with it until you think you have learned it well enough that you won't start mixing up the instructions.

2. Don't try to learn at one time all the commands offered by a software package. Start with some of the simpler functions; move on only when you feel you have a good grasp of those functions.
3. Pick a simple application to try on the software. It doesn't necessarily have to be a business application, but it should be something familiar so that you can easily identify any problems. Balance your checkbook on your financial management system; put your Christmas card list into your file management system; write a letter to everyone you know using word processing.
4. Do all the planning and design work outlined in the previous chapter before you try to implement an application. "Winging it" just doesn't work—at least not well. Having a report neatly laid out with columns and headings will make it much easier to communicate with the report-writing function of your system.
5. Don't be afraid to experiment. You will be surprised at what you learn. You may find an instruction that wasn't in the manual or a different way to use the software.
6. Don't attempt a major project until you are proficient with enough of the software features to carry the whole job through. Practice on minor applications first.

The next section will help you get started with your word processor. Word processing systems are very similar, so it is easier to generalize about how they function. It is also the one software package you are sure to use. However, follow the same approach when you learn any other software.

9.2

GETTING STARTED IN WORD PROCESSING

Whether as a separate system or as part of an integrated package, in all likelihood you will have word processing capability. Some word processors are fairly simple; others cover every writing contingency imaginable. Accept from the beginning that it may take you a long time to become proficient. You are literally learning a new language. Even so, you can make use of a word processing system almost immediately. Furthermore, even that limited use will give you word processing power that's far beyond the capacity of a typewriter.

Use a notebook or index cards to extract some information from your manuals; put the information in some central place where you can refer to it easily. Now write down how your word processing system does the following:

- How do you bring up the master menu and select the edit function?
- How do you end the edit function when you are finished?
- How do you enter the name of the file you want to edit?
- How do you save the file you have edited?
- How do you move the cursor forward and backward one letter at a time? Check your keyboard to see if it has left and right arrow cursor control keys. If it does, use those keys to move the cursor.
- How do you move the cursor up and down one line at a time? Check for cursor control keys again: up and down arrows.
- How do you delete a character?

That's all you need to know to get started in word processing. With those instructions you can do everything you can do with a typewriter, and faster—except printing anything. Now go through all the steps to bring up a file under your own file name and start typing in words. Practice the cursor movements and the delete instruction. Remember, unless you have a very primitive word processing system, you will not have to use the RETURN key at the end of each line, only at the ends of paragraphs.

For the next session, read your manual about the way to print a document. This may be a little confusing if there are many optional ways of printing. Right now, stick to the simple procedure of sending your text directly to the printer in exactly the form you used when you entered it on the screen. Write down that procedure on the index cards or in the notebook. Try to print the text you wrote from the previous day. You are now in business. You can put text into your system, change it, and print it. Everything beyond that is gravy.

But don't stop here. Practice each day and add one or two new instructions. Concentrate on the edit instructions only. Don't bother with the bells and whistles of document formatting until you are proficient with the edit instructions. Work first on the cursor movements: Move it a word at a time, a line at a time, to the end of the paragraph, to the end of the document, and back again. Then work on the delete instructions and so on.

9.3

YOUR OPERATING SYSTEM

Your operating system makes all the other software in your system work. Most of the time you will not be aware of what your operating system is doing. But there will be occasions when you will have to use the services of your operating system directly. Your operating system documentation can be pretty intimidating—you'll find a lot more in there than you need to know. You'll also find more than you ever wanted to know about the functions you will want to use, in a form that will be totally unintelligible to you.

Since operating systems deal mainly with files, let me clear up some terminology and some conventions. To a computer, all things on disks are "files." The file may contain a chapter of your book, a program, or your accounting expenses. Files have names; a program name is simply its file name (just like the file name given to your client file), only it is an *executable* file—that is, a file of instructions that tells the computer how to perform certain functions. The extension in the file name is what usually tells the computer which is which. (Remember that an extension consists of the 3 characters following the period in the file name.) Executable files are referenced without their extensions, while data files must be referenced using their full names. Also, most operating systems, at least the ones I am covering here, do not care if your letters are upper or lower case or mixed.

These are the operating system functions you will want to use.

- Directory: Your operating system allows you to see which files are on any given disk. You need this if your external label is not accurate or to determine the exact name of a file if you can't remember it.
- Disk Status: This command will tell you how large your files are and how much room is left on your disk. Always check this before taking on a large project.
- Formatting: When you buy new disks, you have to format them so they can be read by your system.
- Copy Disk: Sometimes you will back up by copying the entire contents of one disk to another disk.
- Copy File: There will be times when you will want to move files around—either to another disk for backup or on the same disk.
- Listing Files: You can always use your word processor to list text files, but you will not get a listing of the file exactly as it is on the

disk. Your operating system allows you to read any text file, and do it more quickly than on your word processor.

- Delete File: Once you are finished with a file, you may want to get rid of it. Files have a habit of cluttering up your disks.
- Rename File: Occasionally you may want to change the name of a file to something more appropriate or easier to remember.

What I cover in this section applies to the CP/M and MS-DOS (PC-DOS to you IBM users) operating systems. These are the most popular. If you are using another operating system, your commands might be different, but the functions will still be there.

When you first boot your system and bring up your operating system, you see an A> prompt. Whenever you see this A> with the cursor next to it, you know you are communicating directly with the operating system. To use any software, you have to enter a command word to bring up your software. Once you are communicating with the software, there will be a command that allows you to go back to the operating system. If it doesn't or if you have a problem, you can always return to the operating system by pushing the reset button and rebooting the system.

Your software and your operating system functions are programs. When you issue a command under your operating system, you give it the file name of that program. These programs have special file names that tell the operating system that this is a program file and not a data file, and that it is to be executed.

You can recognize program file names by their extensions. Two typical name extensions are COM, and EXE. So your word processing edit program may have a file name of WORDEDIT.COM. To execute that program, you would enter after A> WORDEDIT—the extension is left off. This is the same way you use your operating system functions. Each function is a separate program under a command file name. So if you want to execute the copy function that is in a file called COPY.COM, you would simply enter after the A> COPY.

The operating system always defaults to the "A" or first disk drive when the A> is on the screen. If you want to address any other disk drive, such as the B drive, you have to tell this to the operating system. Much of your other software will expect you to do this also. This is usually accomplished by inputting the drive code followed by a colon before the file name. For example, B:MYFILE.TXT would tell the operating system to look for MYFILE.TXT on disk drive B. You do not have to designate the drive code for the default drive, which is usually drive A.

The first operating system command you will use is the directory. This command gives you a list of the files that are on the disk. Put the operating system into the A drive and enter after the A prompt DIR. You will get a list of all the files on the disk in that drive. The extensions will be separated from the file names by a space, but you will always reference them by using a dot and no spaces. Most operating systems will let you "toggle on" the printer by entering CTRL-P. Enter CTRL-P and then A>DIR. The directory will now print on your printer. (If the system hangs up, it's because you forgot to turn on your printer. Push reset.) You can toggle off the printer by entering CTRL-P again. If you want to see what files are on drive B, you will have to indicate the B drive as DIR B:.

Under MS-DOS, the DIR command will give you some additional information such as the size of the file in bytes. If you want to know more about the disk, perhaps the amount of room left on it, you will have to use the command CHKDSK. Under CP/M, the command is STAT; that will give you the file size as well as the space left. The commands may be followed by the drive code or by a specific file name, such as A>STAT B: or A>STAT B:MYFILE.TXT. Use STAT or CHKDSK often if you are working on a big project and don't want to run out of disk space.

When you get new diskettes, you need to format them. For MS-DOS you will enter the command of A>FORMAT B: and then just follow the instructions on the screen. Under CP/M you will enter the command A>COPY, follow the instructions, and then select the "BLANK" option. If you actually want to make a disk-to-disk copy instead of formatting a blank disk, you would select option "COPY." MS-DOS has a separate command for making disk copies: DISKCOPY.

If you want to copy a file to a new name on a disk or to another disk, you use the command PIP under CP/M. PIP stands for Peripheral Interchange Program. If you want to copy a file from a disk on drive A to a disk on drive B, you would enter a command of:

A>PIP B:NEWFILE.TXT = **ORGFILE.TXT**

Note that the original file is on the right side of the = and the copy file is on the left side. If both files have the same name and you get confused, you could overwrite your original with the old copy.

If you are a MS-DOS user, your command to copy individual files is "COPY." You accomplish the same copy as above by entering:

A>COPY ORGFILE.TXT B:NEWFILE.TXT

Note that the files are reversed—the receiving file is on the right side. If you are using a computer with dual processors and you are using both operating systems, be careful.

The ability to display any file can be handy for seeing exactly what it is. You merely have to enter the command A>TYPE B:MYFILE.TXT and everything in that file will scroll up your screen at lightning speed. Toggle on your printer, and it all will be printed for you.

Two more operating system commands are the *deleting* and *re-*

naming capabilities. To delete a file, use the command "ERASE" (ERA in CP/M). Make sure you want to delete that particular file and check your file name spelling carefully. Once you issue this command, your file, as far as you are concerned, is gone forever. The "RENAME" (REN under CP/M) command allows you to change the names of files. Under MS-DOS this command would be:A>RENAME OLDNAME.TXT NEWNAME.TXT

Note: the new file name is on the right. In CP/M this command would be:

A>REN NEWNAME.TXT=**OLDNAME.TXT**

Under CP/M the new file name is on the left, but in the renaming function you do not have to worry about confusing the format. If you make a mistake, the operating system will merely come back with a question mark, because it will not be able to find NEWNAME.TXT on the disk.

That is really all you need to know to handle your own work on the operating system. Once you have become comfortable with your system, you may want to read a little bit more about these commands and others in your operating system's reference manual. For the time being, just stick with the above. You have enough things to cope with right now.

9.4

CONFIGURING YOUR FILES

After a while you may notice you spend a lot of time changing disks. Not only is this tiresome, but it may also cause you to put off important chores, like backing up your files, because it is just too much trouble to change all those disks.

Your software is probably organized so that each program is on a separate disk. That is how it came when you bought it, so that is how you have kept it. Now that you have some idea of how your operating system works, you can make some changes and eliminate some of those disk-changing problems.

List out the directories of all your software disks and see if you can identify the function of each command file (look for extensions such as COM or EXE). These command files might make use of some of the other files, but you will not be able to tell. The name might give you a clue, so see if you can identify the files being used by the command files.

Now go back to your procedures. Identify what software you use for each type of job you do. For instance, you might frequently have to use your file management and word processing systems together. You only need the edit program from your word processor, because the mail generator does all the printing. Look at the files on your file management disk. There will be some that were used to originally create the database. You used them once and probably won't ever use them again for this particular file. You also have a report generator program that you do not need for your mail generation. Copy the word processing edit and the file management functions you need for your mail generation onto a new formatted disk. Now you have everything conveniently on one disk. Always copy your needed files over to a new disk and leave your original software disk the way it was.

In another situation, you might be doing a lot of writing, and you would be regularly checking your disk space, copying backups, and counting words, as well as using all the features of your word processor system. So you need all the facilities of your word processor, plus the copy and disk status commands from your operating system and the word-count capability from your spelling system so you don't have to constantly use three disks. The problem is that your word processing takes up all the room on your A drive disk. There is no reason why you can't put these files on the B drive disk where you are putting your text. You won't fill it up as long as you regularly check its status. Just remember that in order to use them, you must use the B: in front of the command file name. For example, under CP/M, you would check the file status as A>B:STAT B:MYFILE.TXT.

Sit down with some of your own situations and see if you can improve your own working disk configurations. Before you start moving too many files around, find out the size of each file by using your operating system's file status command. That way, you can do a little arithmetic to see if all the files will fit on your new disk.

9.5

YOUR WORKING DOCUMENTATION

No matter how good or poor the documentation is that came with your software, once you begin using your software, you will want to make up your own documentation.

Get yourself a looseleaf notebook and some dividers with tabs, labeling them as follows:

- Commands: This is the reference section of your documentation. Set up a different page or section for each type of software you work with. These sections will include everything from your word processing edit commands to your operating system utility commands.
- File Definitions: If you have created files, using your file management system, you will want to define each field in the file.

- Sample Reports: A sample of every report put out by your report generator.
- Sample Forms: Samples of all those form letters or preprinted forms you collected early in your design activities.
- Procedures: Your work-flow procedures. You will want a separate page or section for each type of work activity you do.
- Special Reference Listing: Included in this section are the special lists you will need to reference in your everyday work, such as listings of the contents of disks and master file listings such as clients by client number. This is one section of your manual that will be updated frequently.

When you set up your command section, select only those commands that you will be using. No need to clutter up your working manual with any others. Group the commands in a way that is meaningful to you. Make up your own definitions and examples if you feel that would help remind you of what the command is used for and how to use it. If you use a series of commands in a special sequence, show that sequence. For instance, there may be a series of commands needed to use multiple screens. Label it "multiple screens" and write down the sequence of commands.

For the file definitions, go back to the work sheets you prepared when you first designed the files. Set up a separate section in your file definitions for each type of record. For each field in that record, put down the prompt, field length, type of data (numeric, and so on), edit rules, any codes and what they mean, special formatting (dates), and, if appropriate, the "tag" name. (See the Data List example in Chapter 8.) Include a sample printout of the screen format if you can. You will refer back to the file definitions if you ever forget what is included in a field, or forget what name you gave to a field when you are preparing form letters.

The report section will include a sample of every report printed as part of your system. At the top of every report sample, write the system and program or file name that produces it. If you end up with a lot of reports, this will help you locate the one you need. You will also be able to see if the report has the data you are looking for. Include in this section a sample of any spreadsheet output. Write on the top of each spreadsheet sample its file name and disk number. This way, when you want to use a spreadsheet, you can identify the one you want to use, and you will know where it is.

Remember all those sample form letters you gathered in your planning stage? Print each one of them out, and if they are set up to work with a mail generator, print them out in that form. Also, print out samples of any preprinted forms and indicate the alignment right on the sample. You tend to forget if you don't use something frequently. On each sample, write the file name and the number of the disk. You now have a place where you can look at every form letter and find its location quickly.

In the section on "work flow," you developed procedures for each of your primary functions. At that point it was only a general outline of what steps you needed to accomplish a job. When it came time to interface with the computer, you only wrote down something general like "Enter client into the file management system." Now you want to be a little more specific. Let's say that "Enter client into the file management system" was item 11 in your work-flow procedures. You might expand your instructions as follows:

11. Enter client into the file management system.

A. Put disk 36, WEDDING CLIENTS, into drive B.

B. Enter "MENU"

C. Select "D. UPDATE"

D. Enter file "B:WEDCLNT.FLE"

E. Select "C. ADD A NEW RECORD"

F. Enter data:
   1) Enter assigned key in CLIENT NUMBER LOG
   2) Code STATUS as *N* for new

G. Enter CTRL-E to end update

Follow this example for each interface with the computer systems. Some detail instructions may also be necessary for some of your other systems. *Note:* in the above example I did not go into the detail coding of the client record except where it was unique to this kind of entry. This information is already covered in the file definition section of your personal documentation.

The last section of your notebook is one that you will update frequently. It will contain your own working listings. Include here a listing of the contents of each disk. Use your operating system "DIR" with the printer on or, better yet, use the utility that includes the size of the files. Write the disk number on the listing Periodically, you will want to review this list and mark the files to be deleted. Include all your master file lists. You may have an alphabetical list of clients that gives their client numbers. Or you may have a master list of all your photos. Make sure you have a master list of each one of your files showing the key and some other identifying information. This is especially important if you access the file by name. If you can't remember exactly how you put that name in, you may have a lot of trouble retrieving that record. Remember these machines are precise—and dumb.

Developing your working documentation itself is a learning procedure. Once you have developed it, you may not have to refer to it all the time, but there will be times, especially if you do not do a procedure frequently, when you will be glad it is there. It also will be invaluable if you ever have someone else help you with your work. And one final note: It will be the tangible form of your system, something you can show people and something that you yourself can look at and be proud of.

Congratulations! You have successfully completed your computer system.

10

THE PHOTO NETWORKS

Welcome to the exciting world of telecommunications! If you haven't been thinking about using your computer to link into the information networks, you will be in the very near future. The communication networks will have a significant influence on the way photography business is conducted.

What is a network? It's merely a group of connected communication devices. You're already connected into two networks in your home via your TV set and telephone. In a data communications network, computers are hooked up to each other via telephone lines so they can "talk" to each other. This allows instant transmission of information across the street, the country, or the world. And, of course, computers do this very fast. You can communicate directly with other people via their computers; you can access data from the big information utilities; you can get everything from "want lists" to camera equipment from those networks specifically designed for computerized photographers.

Even if you decide that you do not need a computer to handle your everyday business, you may want to get a computer if only to enable you to use the networks. If you already own an inexpensive computer, you could use it for this purpose. While you need a fairly sophisticated system to handle your business, you really only need a small, hand-held computer or a simple terminal to be able to communicate with the networks. However, there is so much material in these information networks that you will probably want a full computer system so you can store and print all that information on your own system.

When you enter the world of telecommunications, you leave the world of digital computers. Computers must conform to the rules of the communication network, and if you can believe it, communications jargon is worse than the computer jargon. There are new words and new concepts that must be learned if you are going to be able to choose and use the proper equipment.

10.1

GOING ON-LINE

"Going on-line" means connecting your computer to a communications network—your telephone line. This is fairly simple to do except that your computer talks digital (discrete bits) and your telephone line talks in sound waves (continuous tones). The transition from one to the other is accomplished by the modem.

In an on-line network situation, your computer becomes a "dumb" terminal under the control of a sophisticated mainframe computer at some other location. All the storage, files, software, and processing are with this mainframe computer. Your computer has no real power except to send and receive information from this big computer.

I will go into this in more detail, but to go on-line you will need:

- A *serial* port. (Serial ports were discussed in Chapter 5, Selecting a Computer.) Lacking a serial port, you will have to purchase a plug-in communications card.
- A *modem* or modulator/demodulator (introduced in Chapter 2), which converts the digital signals of your computer into the voice-grade signals of your telephone and back again.
- A *cable* to hook your computer to the modem.
- *Communications software* that will turn your computer into a dumb terminal and handle some of the housekeeping chores of telecommunications.
- And, of course, a *telephone line.*

When I first talked about computers, I discussed how computers represent data by off/on signals called bits, and how these bits were grouped together in groups of eight called bytes. Now, normally, whenever a computer transfers these bits, it does so eight bits at a time. This is called *parallel transmission*, because all eight bits are transferred simultaneously. When data are sent through telephone lines, they can't be transferred as eight bits abreast but must be sent one bit at a time. This is called *serial transmission*. In order for your computer to transmit its data in this mode, it must have a serial port. Most of the newer computers are equipped with a serial port as standard equipment. If your computer does not have a serial port, then you will have to purchase a plug-in communications card with an RS-232C (or RS-232) interface.

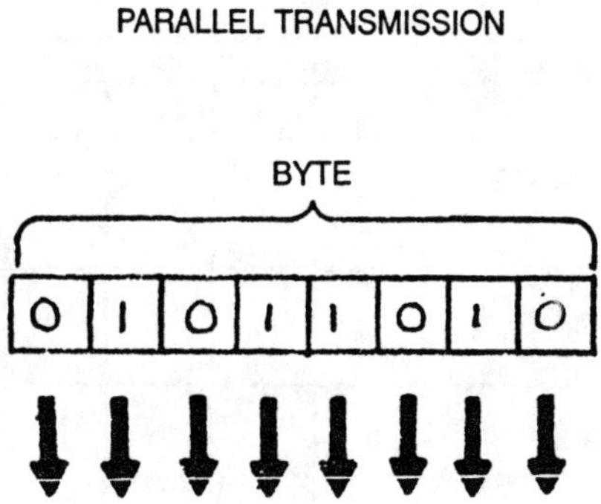

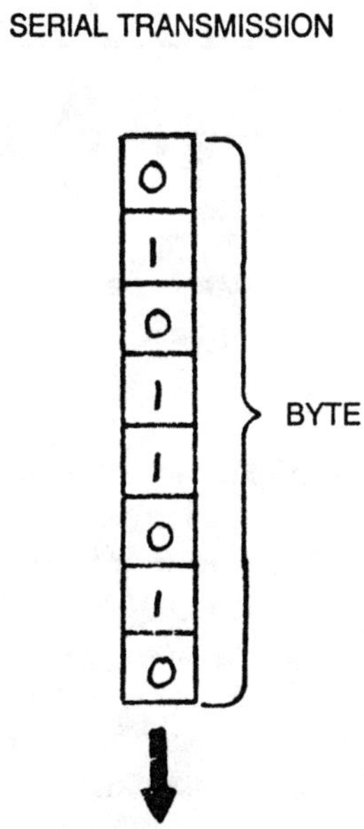

10-A. Parallel and Serial Transmission

The second piece of equipment your computer will need is a modem. The modem transfers the digital data produced by the computer into a form that can be transferred over voice-grade telephone lines, then back into the form understood by the computer. This is accomplished by converting "one" bits into one frequency and "zero" bits into another frequency.

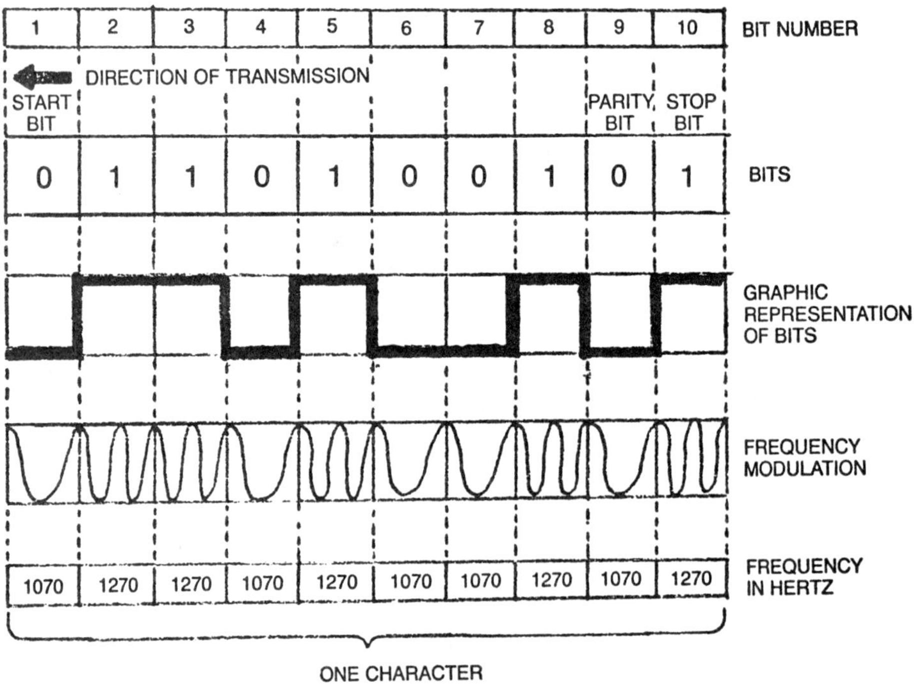

10-B. Conversion of Digital Data to Sound Frequencies

For computers, the basic digital unit is a bit. When we enter the communications media, the transmission rate is measured in what is called *bauds* or *baud rate.* Baud is a term left over from the early telegraph days; for all purposes, it is equivalent to the number of bits. Modems for microprocessors usually come in two-baud rates: *300 baud* or *1200 baud.* You will want a modem that transfers at a 300-baud rate. A 1200-baud modem is four times as fast but costs twice the money of a 300-baud-rate modem. Also, networks often charge extra for using the faster 1200-baud rate. A fast typist types 8-10 characters per second. The 300-baud modem transfers at a speed of 30 characters per second. If you are printing or transferring to disk massive amounts of data, then a 1200-baud modem may be justified. Just make sure your 1200-baud modem also gives you the 300-baud option. All networks support the 300-baud rate.

In telecommunications transmissions, ten bits are usually transmitted, so when you translate your baud rate to characters, you will divide by ten. The two extra bits are the start and stop bits that signal the beginning and end of the character transmission. The start bit is a zero, and the ending bit is a one.

Modems can be *half-duplex* and *full-duplex*. With half-duplex, communication travels in one direction at a time, much like the CB radio operator who talks, says "over," then lets the other person talk, and so on. A signal is sent from one computer to another and must be completed before the other computer can send one back. With full-duplex, communication is a two-way street, and the signals go back and forth simultaneously, similar to talking on the telephone. A full-duplex modem allows the receiving computer to constantly verify the transmission and ask that something be sent again if there is a problem. You will want a modem with both half- and full-duplex capabilities.

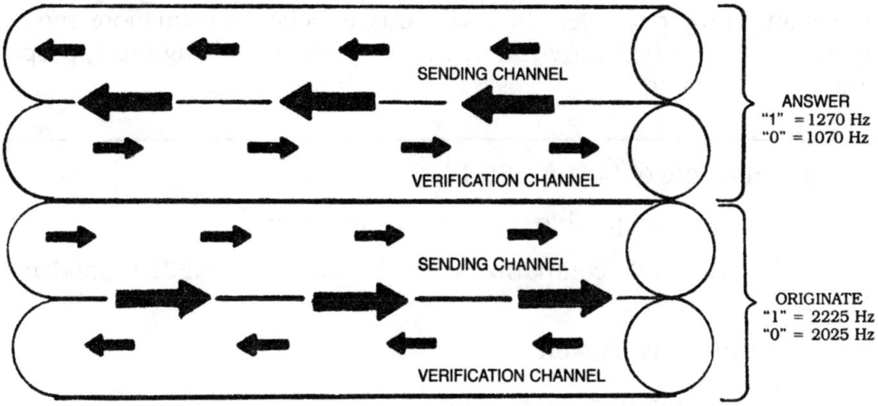

10-C. Communications Channels

Your modem will also have two settings: "originate" mode and "answer" mode. The terms actually have arbitrary meanings and only refer to the two communications channels. When you are on-line to a network, you will set your modem to the "originate" channel. If you are communicating with another friend, you will have to agree as to who will use the "answer" channel and who will use the "originate" channel.

Modems developed by the telephone company set the standard in the industry, so make sure the modem you buy meets these standards. A 300-baud modem with answer and originate capabilities should be compatible with the Bell System 103. A 1200-baud modem that can communicate in either 300- or 1200-baud, in either full- or half-duplex, should be compatible with the Bell 212A.

Two other terms you will hear when you deal with the communications media are *synchronous* and *asynchronous.* In *synchronous transmission,* the bits flow in a continuous transmission; the beginning and end of a byte are determined by precise timing. In *asynchronous transmission,* the beginning and end of a byte are determined by special start and stop bits. You will want an asynchronous modem, since all the services that you'll use will transmit in this mode.

Modems come in two types: *direct-connect* and those with *acoustic couplers.* At one time there was a big price difference, but now there isn't, so buy a direct-connect modem. This modem plugs directly into your phone line jack. With an acoustic coupler, the headset of the phone is placed into two rubber cups, and the data are transferred through the mouthpiece and earpiece. There is more of a chance that interference in the form of stray noise can happen in the acoustic version than in the direct-connect versions. If, however, you are a traveler and use your computer to check with your network while you are on the road, you may prefer an acoustic coupler. That way you can check in from motel rooms, pay phones, or wherever without worrying about finding the appropriate telephone plug.

- Baud rate of 300 or 300/1200
- 300 bps compatible with Bell 103 modems
- 300/1200 bps compatible with Bell 103 and Bell 212A modems, respectively
- Serial transmission
- Asynchronous transmission
- Word length: seven and eight bits
- Stop bits: one and two bits
- Parity: odd, even, or none
- Half-duplex and full-duplex communication
- Both answer/originate capabilities

10-D. Modem Summary

10.2

COMMUNICATIONS SOFTWARE

In order to communicate with a network, your system and the network's system must both be set for the same parameters, usually referred to as *protocol.* Protocol makes sure that both computers are following the same rules when they send and receive data. Some "intelligent" modems will figure out most of the protocol when they make the connection with another computer. With others, you have to set the modem or the communications software to the appropriate protocol. Even though some of this may seem a little foreign to you, you do not have to understand everything, since the network will tell you what to do. Protocol rules include the following:

- Full- or half-duplex
- Baud rate
- Word length (usually seven bits)
- Parity: odd, even, or none (used to check for transmission errors)
- Number of stop bits
- Echo on (characters will be reflected on your screen)
- Modem setting (usually originate)

All communications software should allow you to set the communications protocol, but there are some other features that will be quite useful to you. The minimum monthly fee you'll be charged by most networks probably translates to one hour of computer connect time per month. If you check with your network just ten times a month, this only allows you six minutes a session to browse around. Chances are you will need a lot more time, and this adds up to a lot of money very quickly. Many communications software programs allow you to *download* data. That is, when you find something worthwhile, you can transfer it to your computer memory and save it on your disk in very little time. You can then review it at your leisure without running up your connect time.

Another alternative is to be able to *toggle* on your printer when you see something on the screen that interests you so that you can have a hard copy to study once you are off-line. The opposite of "download" is *upload.* This allows you to sit at your computer off-line and take all the time you want in creating a file, and then to transfer it quickly to the network storage facility or to someone else's computer while on-line.

Two other useful features are a *timer* (to remind you of how long you have been on the network) and an *auto-log-on.* When you establish contact with another computer, you normally give your account number and password. This is called *log-on* (or *sign-on*) and can take a bit of time. The log-on is always the same. You give the log-on instructions to your communications software; thereafter, the auto-log-on does it for you. *Note:* when you quit a system, you *log off* or *sign off;* it is usually a single-word entry.

There are many features found in communications software, and programmers are inventing new little goodies every day. Have your computer salesperson explain each feature and how you might use it, and then you decide if it would be useful to you. Chances are the ones described above will be all you will really need. More features may only confuse you.

10.3

ELECTRONIC MAIL

Electronic mail is the sending of a message from one computer to another via the communications network. You can establish telephone contact with the computer of a friend, and what you type on your keyboard appears on his monitor screen. This is not really practical, since you could talk to him faster on the phone. Most likely what you would do is prepare a letter first and store it on a disk, then call him up and transmit the letter to his disk file. At his leisure he could either read your letter on his monitor or print it on his own printer.

Actually, if you have the proper software, neither of you needs to even be there. Let's say you are collaborating with a friend on a book—you are in Los Angeles, and he is in New York. You want to send him a revised copy of the manuscript, but even at your computer's high-speed transmission it will take a healthy bit of telephone time. So you decide to send it after 11 p.m. when the rates are lower. But you also want to go to a party that night. He, on the other hand, will be receiving it after 2 a.m., when he would prefer to be fast asleep. No problem: Just leave the proper instructions with your computer, and at the time you specify, your computer will automatically call his computer, exchange information, and hang up.

Many of the national networks offer "mailbox" services where other subscribers can leave messages with each other. If you are constantly on the road, you know how difficult it is for people to reach you. This way you can check into your mailbox from anywhere in the world. Let's say you are collaborating with another photographer on an assignment. You are traveling separately, and you have no idea where the other will be, but you have to stay in touch with each other. Normally, you would have to arrange a time and place for communication, which could really hinder your schedule. But now, thanks to the electronic mailbox, you can communicate with each other anytime. Also, if your client suddenly has to reach you and no one knows where you are, your electronic mailbox comes to the rescue.

Even if your recipient is not tied into any sort of communications network, you can still use your computer to get mail to him faster. Many networks offer a service where they receive your electronic communication, have it printed, and delivered to the recipient. MCI Mail, Photonet Express, and other such services offer this convenience. Even the post office offers a computer-originated mail service, E-COM, which requires a minimum of two hundred recipients. You transmit your letter and the two hundred or more addresses to the post office service center. The post office prints the letter, addresses the envelopes, and completes the hand delivery—promised within twenty-four hours.

10.4

NATIONAL NETWORKS

The national networks are great information services. They have been used by big businesses for years, but now there are many that are designed for smaller businesses and individual users. As research facilities, they can't be beat. You can find almost anything, and they are as up-to-date as possible. Many of the larger networks offer special services for photographers. At this writing there are two that are especially designed to provide information and services for freelance photographers. These are *Photo-1* and *Photonet.*

If your business could benefit from these services, I would strongly recommend them, since they can put you way ahead of your competition. But before you leap into the world of data communications and national networks, first consider the cost, which can be quite considerable. You will have to evaluate these costs in terms of the benefit to your business:

- The cost of the modem and communications software. This will run you at least three hundred dollars—and probably more—depending upon the level of sophistication you require.
- The sign-up fee to join a network. Sometimes there are situations where you can get this initial sign-up fee waived as part of a promotional campaign of some equipment manufacturer. Otherwise, this fee can be as high as one hundred dollars.

- There is usually a minimal monthly charge, whether you use the system or not. This can be a pretty hefty sum for a system you never use, so make sure you will use it.
- Telephone costs. You have to pay the price of the telephone call, although there are usually "free" lines or reduced-cost lines you can use. The free line is not really free, since its cost will be built into the connect-time fee, explained below.
- The connect-time fee is the actual charge for using the services of the network, usually charged by the minute or fractions of an hour. Since those minutes add up very fast, the bills can get surprisingly high.
- Other costs that you should consider that may or may not be charged by your network are sign-on charges, storage charges, surcharges for accessing certain databases, and charges for using a fast (1200-baud) transfer rate.

Read the following sections on the available networks. If you feel that one will be really valuable in your business, then an on-line system will be worthwhile for you. If not, remember that it can be a very expensive undertaking, so make sure you evaluate all the costs before you take on a system for "nice-to-have" reasons.

10.4.1 Photonet

The first photographic network was Photonet, which started offering its services to photographers and picture buyers on a regular basis in September 1983. Its main purpose is to provide business services for the photographer plus a centralized area where the buyers and sellers of photographs can get together to communicate their needs and services. Photonet also provides special services to picture buyers and researchers in order to attract them to the network. This assures you, as a photographer, that there will be many potential clients available through the system.

Photonet is available at all hours, seven days a week. It can be reached by a local phone number from 130 cities in the United States, Canada, England, and France. In addition, there is an 800 number. The only expenses in using Photonet are the initial sign-up fee of forty-nine dollars and the connect time charge of twenty-four dollars per hour, the minimum charge per month. If you are serious about selling your photography and are trying to reach a nationwide market, then Photonet is well worth it. The services offered can save you hours of letter writing and put you immediately in touch with national and international clients' picture needs, as well as give you a place where you can advertise your pictures or services.

When you sign on to Photonet, you are presented with the main menu, which defines the particular services available on the network. These services include the following:

- Communications
- News and Information
- Photographic Agencies
- Photo Research Directory
- The Marketplace
- Manufacturer's Professional Services

Under "Communications" the first item is "Electronic Mail." This allows you to communicate with other photographers and clients directly on the system. If you read a client's want list and have the photo needed, you can notify that client immediately that you have what he needs. If you are traveling and notice that a client needs to have some pictures taken in your location, you can let him know you are available. The clients in turn can send a message to you acknowledging interest in either your pictures or service. The communication is very swift, and you do not have to be tied to your mailbox to get the messages. As soon as you sign on to Photonet, you are informed of any messages that are waiting for you. All messages are private and can be read only by you.

What if you have to get a letter to someone who doesn't have a computer? You can use Photonet Express. When you send the letter or document via Photonet Express, it is printed on Photonet Express stationery and hand delivered by messenger within two hours. You can receive confirmation of delivery either by written receipt or by a notice on electronic mail. This service is available for delivery in many U.S. cities. The cost of a Photonet Express letter is twelve dollars, but if you need to get mail to someone immediately, it is the fastest service available.

The regional bulletin boards are for personal use and contain three sections: "For Sale," "Wanted," and "Notices." Use the "For Sale" if you want to sell some photography equipment or are in the market for some used gear. It is also a good place to find software specifically designed for photographic purposes. The "Wanted" section is where you might post some equipment you are looking for or, as some photographers do, post the need for some information. Responses to these bulletin board requests can be made via electronic mail. "Notices" can be anything. Sometimes they are agencies looking for photographers or photographers announcing their travel plans.

The final item under the "Communications" heading is "Photonet Feedback." This is your link with the Photonet service; you can use it if you have a problem with your bill or service, need some questions answered, or just have a good idea that you want to pass on to Photonet.

The next item in the Photonet menu is "News and Information." The categories on this section will help you stay current with what is happening in the photographic industry. Photonet publishes its own newsletter, in which you will find timely articles on what is going on with stock photography, marketing, legal issues, equipment, new photographic methods, plus the new services being offered by Photonet.

In addition to its own newsletter, Photonet publishes additional newsletters and magazines under the "Industry Publications" category. These include popular consumer magazines as well as industry-specific newsletters. Except for the connect-time fee, many of them are free for you to read.

The "Copyright Database/Information Request" section allows you to review copyright information and see what government publications are available. If you are interested in any of the publications or copyright forms, you can order them directly from Photonet.

Under the heading "New Equipment and Supplies," you will find a brief description of the latest in cameras, lenses, studio equipment, darkroom needs, accessories, video equipment, computers, and software. Check this area as well as the regional "For Sale" bulletin board if you are looking for photographic equipment or software. If you want additional information on any item, your request is automatically forwarded to the manufacturer.

Under "Professional Organizations" there is a mininetwork where various professional organizations can provide their members with newsletter highlights, meeting announcements, and other bulletins. These may be protected by a password for member use only. But even if you are not a member, you can get some information on the organization's services and the membership requirements. The "Public Bulletin Board" in this section enables members of organizations without their own network to post and receive messages.

The photo agency category is also a network unto itself. Agencies are listed by name, and you will find many of the best-known agencies listed here. This mininetwork is actually maintained by the agency itself to provide information for photographers seeking representation, clients looking for new agencies or trying to fill picture requests, and the agency to communicate with its own photographers, especially in the area of providing pictures the agent may not have on file.

Under each agency there are five categories from which to choose. The "Introduction" tells you about the agency and in what type of photography it specializes. The "Photo Guidelines" tell you the procedures to follow if you are interested in submitting pictures. The "Agency Update" may contain the agency's own newsletter, or the agency may post information that would be of interest to its photographers or clients. If you are a photographer seeking representation, you can select the "Request Promotional Material" category and automatically be sent material about the agency.

The final heading is "Needed Photographs." This may be protected by password so that only the photographers under contract with the agency can read the requests, or the agency may request that any noncontract photographer who wants to submit pictures contact the agency first. Under this category, the agencies list their outstanding current picture needs.

"The Photo Research Directory" is the business end of the system. This is where researchers, agencies, and buyers list their picture needs and where you can post your pictures, services, and travel itineraries.

If you have just returned from a trip or have shot some special pictures, you can list your picture subjects under "Stock Update—New Images" under "The Photo Research Directory." If you are planning on taking a trip and would like to notify prospective clients of your travel plans, you can post your itineraries under "Travel Update—Itineraries." If you are looking for markets for your stock photography or are looking for assignments, then you will want to check the listings under "Stock Photography Requests" or "Assignment Photography Requests."

How about a place where you can advertise your photographic services and specialties? Photonet has that, too, in the form of the "Subscriber/Photo Sources Database." Here you can list your name, address, phone number, associations with which you're affiliated, photographic specialty, special services you offer, types of pictures you have on file, and so on. Quickly and conveniently, a client can access this directory and find the match he needs for his project.

The next item in the master menu is "Resources and Services." These are special services directly available to you that might be useful in your photography business. For instance, if you need title slides for a special presentation, you can find services that will produce these for you, and you can order the slides on-line. Or let's say you want to send some promotional material to advertising agencies—you can order mailing lists of all advertising agencies. Check out this section and see what services are available.

The "Photographer's Source" provides nationwide support services for professional photographers. These include rental space and equipment, stylists, model agencies, casting services, assistants, and transportation services.

Other services that may be of interest to the professional photographer are the travel agencies and insurance services. These agencies specialize in the needs of the photographer and are available on-line.

The "Manufacturers Professional Services" is another area you might want to look into. Are you far from home when your Nikon breaks down? Contact Nikon professional services on-line for help or listing of repair shops in your vicinity. Scan the list of services in this area to find out what is available before you go elsewhere for help.

The "Marketplace" is a shop-by-computer service for photographers. You can shop for equipment, accessories, and supplies at discount prices. Everything can be ordered directly on-line and charged to your credit card. If your purchases are over one hundred dollars, you even get a two-dollar credit against your connect time.

Photonet provides many services and is constantly adding new ones, so I am only able to give you a sample. If you think you might be interested in Photonet, contact them for more up-to-date information. You will find their address listed in Appendix B.

10.4.2 Photo-1

At the time of this writing, Photo-1 was not yet fully operational. Photo-1 developed out of a special need to communicate with many professional photographers on assignment. The developers of the system were on a special project in Australia trying to coordinate the activities of many freelance professionals and began using a computer system as a communications vehicle. The project eventually developed into a network service to aid professional photographers with similar problems.

Photo-1 plans to be more specialized than Photonet. Although Photo-1 offers similar services such as electronic mail, bulletin boards, equipment and stock photo needs, its services are specifically designed for the well-established professional photojournalist. In addition, it offers conferencing, scheduling, marketing information, and press-credential services specifically tailored to the needs of photojournalists.

Contact Photo-1 for more current information on what the network has to offer to find out if it is suitable for your type of photographic business.

10.4.3 The Generalized Networks

Besides the specialized photographic networks, there are many other nationwide networks. The general information networks may be of interest to you if you need some research facilities. Some of the networks that are specialized for a specific group, or that provide bulletin board services for special groups, may also be of interest to you if you specialize in a certain industry. For instance, if you specialize in agricultural subjects or aviation, you might see if there is a network offering services to those industries, and then post your services on one of their bulletin boards. There are so many networks that it is impossible to list them all, but there are some general information networks set up for individuals or small businesses that might be of some interest to you.

- After business hours, the expensive and very sophisticated Bibliographic Retrieval Services becomes the less expensive BRS/After Dark. BRS/After Dark is designed for individual and business users who occasionally need information from its more than twenty databases.

- One of the more popular networks is CompuServe. It was originally established for computer hobbyists who wanted access to sophisticated software and needed more storage facilities than they had on their machines. Now it is a full-fledged information network offering databases in business, travel, and consumer interests.

- Delphi by General Videotex offers electronic mail, subject bulletin boards, library services, and consumer and business databases.

- As you can guess, the Dow Jones News/Retrieval Service has business information. But it has a great deal more, including the complete text of the Academic American Encyclopedia and Electronic Catalog Shopping.

- Like BRS/After Dark, the Knowledge Index is an after-hours information service from Dialog Information Services. It offers twelve major databases for those needing research facilities.

- NewsNet offers the full text of some 150 newsletters in more than forty different business categories. It also offers electronic mail services.

- The original, and probably the largest, information network designed for the small user is The Source. It features many databases of interest to businesses or individuals. It also has travel information and services, electronic mail, about seventy-five subject bulletin boards, shopping services, and a special user electronic publishing section.

10.5

LOCAL SERVICES AND BULLETIN BOARDS

Local area networks differ from the national networks in that they do not supply national toll-free numbers, and their areas of interest are purely regional. The local network in which you as a photographer would be most interested is the "Electronic Yellow Pages." If you are a local wedding photographer, the national networks can't help you in securing business, but a local electronic yellow pages would. They are searched by keywords such as "PHOTOGRAPHER, WEDDING." You can keep your listing up-to-date on a daily basis if you wish.

Bulletin board services (BBS) are maintained by individuals or small businesses. Most are run by dealers, computer clubs, or user groups. They are usually free and offer shopping services, a place for individuals to exchange information, or free public-domain software. They are maintained by individual operators called *sysop* (system operators), are usually on a microcomputer system, and can handle only one caller at a time. If you hunt around, you will find some devoted to photography.

You can set up your own BBS. It could be a forum whereby photographers exchange leads and information. If you have a rather extensive and frequently changing stock file, you could post your file on your bulletin board; picture buyers and photo researchers with computers and communications capabilities could scan your file when they are looking for pictures. You could collaborate with other photographers and combine stock lists on your bulletin board or even turn it into a miniagency. You could provide lead services to other photographers. All this can be open to anyone who calls, or available only to those who have a password to log on to the system, with or without a fee.

What do you need to set up your own BBS? A computer of at least 16K, reliable disk drives, an auto-answer modem, a telephone line, and some BBS software. You will then have to decide what services you want to offer, the hours of the day you want to be operational, and if you are going to restrict access to your system. Once you set up a BBS, you have to make it available on a regular basis so that people who might use it can depend on it. If you do not want to tie up your business computer, you may wish to purchase a second, less expensive computer. Simple home computers are quite suitable for this type of service.

11 THE FUTURE

The electronic digital computer has been around for only forty years. It has been commercially available for only thirty years. And it has been affordable for individuals and small businesses for less than ten years. Progress toward information automation was very slow at first, but now the computer is an everyday item in our lives. The future, even in the next few years, is very exciting.

11.1 WHAT NEXT?

What does the future hold? Most of the technology covered in this section exists today. The only problem is that new innovations may not yet be commercially feasible or still too expensive for widespread use.

There is no doubt that computers are getting smaller and smaller while at the same time growing more powerful, with tremendous memory capability. Already, 32-bit and 64-bit microprocessors are being developed. Soon it will be commonplace for RAM to be a million bytes. As the small computers solve their data storage problems and allow common access by multiple users and as minicomputers use more and more microcomputer technology, it will become impossible to tell them apart. Even more significant, the powerful and economical microprocessors with their million-byte memories will effect a converging technological evolution between the microcomputers and the mainframe computers used in the big companies. The computers will not only be smaller and better but will be a lot cheaper and will require very little electric power.

The future can be seen developing in the portables. Just a couple of years ago they were nonexistent; now they are everywhere. A lot of research is going into making them smaller and better. Monitors have been the biggest problem. But newer monitors are being developed, and if the resolution and display capabilities are as good as the old, reliable CRT, then the CRT will probably become obsolete. Portables will become more powerful computers rivaling the full-featured machines, and the stay-at-home machines will start looking more like portables. The new definition of a portable will probably be a pocket computer.

Both portables and larger systems are limited by their mass storage capabilities. Floppy disks have been the standard, but their days may be numbered as more and more personal computers start using hard disks. Hard disks are being improved to withstand the rigors of a less-than-ideal environment. Bubble memories have been around for some time; although accessing data on a bubble memory is slower than on a floppy disk, an incredible amount of data can be packed into a very small package. Look for plug-in, matchbook-size cartridges of bubble memory in the future. The laser optical videodisk used in the movie industry is also being developed as a storage medium. Grooves representing the familiar 0's and 1's are read by a light beam, and a single disk can hold a billion bytes of data! Its only drawback is that it cannot be erased, but it still can provide libraries of information.

Computers will become friendlier and easier to use. Already a great deal of effort is being put into developing software that makes using a computer into child's play. No doubt your computer will soon be talking to you. For a few hundred dollars you can get it to talk to you now. Computers can translate keyboard characters into different phonemes or sounds and can audibly produce those sounds. It still sounds a little flat and metallic, but progress is being made.

How about you talking to it? That can be done now, but the process is more complicated. Machines must deal with precise data that must be translated into a digital form. Our language is far from precise. There is also the problem of accents and tonal quality. I have trouble understanding some people's English; imagine the problems of a dumb machine that can only understand bits! The computer can "learn" to interpret an individual person's speech, but the whole thing falls apart if the person catches a cold, which alters his speech. Voice recognition is coming in the near future—but don't start dictating letters to your computer yet.

What about digitized photographs that can be electrically transmitted to your client? That is definitely possible. Our space probes did not take pictures of Jupiter, stick them in a Kodak mailer, and jettison them back to earth. They took high-quality digital photographs that were transmitted back to computers. But the technology is still expensive, and there have to be enough people using and accepting the process before it will be in common use.

Electronic mail will become more commonplace. In fact, most

first-class letters will probably be electronically mailed. Network utilities will become the central source of information; more and more business will be conducted using network communication facilities.

How about a thinking machine? Artificial intelligence has been discussed for decades. The problem is that no one has agreed on a definition of artificial intelligence. Machines can learn; that is, they can alter their programming on the bases of right and wrong actions. The Japanese have committed to a project to develop the "fifth generation" of computers before the decade is out. These machines will be able to reason, draw conclusions, make judgments, and understand both written and spoken words. HAL, are you out there?

11.2

PHOTOGRAPHY AND THE COMPUTER

What does all this mean to the freelance photographer? You are not interested in discussing the finer points of philosophy with your computer. The importance of the computer in your business future is the revolution in communication possible through the computer networks. No longer will you spend days typing up dreary query letters and waiting weeks before the postman brings you a reply. Already the facilities of Photo-1 and Photonet provide a means for clients to instantaneously communicate their photographic needs to the world. As more photographers begin using these facilities, more clients will start publishing their needs on them.

Once the technology of digitizing photographs becomes affordable and acceptable, you will be able to transmit samples of your images instantaneously or maybe put them into a library maintained on a network. Clients can view and choose their pictures without waiting days or weeks for the mail. They will also not have the bother or the risk of handling all those submissions. Eventually, technology will be able to produce fine-resolution digital photographs, and then clients will buy directly through the communications media.

Imagine yourself out taking pictures. A newsworthy event takes place, and you happen to be in the right spot at the right time. You point your digital camera (contained in your watch with your computer) at the scene and take a series of fantastic pictures. You then go to the nearest telephone, call up your agency network, and transmit your pictures into your file. Your agent immediately reroutes them to the news agencies. Your pictures are purchased by several news agencies and immediately published in several printed daily news magazines as well as some electronic ones. You are paid immediately, and all money is instantly transferred to your account. No developing, no hassles, no queries, no waiting, no billing, and no more being tied to an office. Now that's a computerized business!

Appendix A

ASCII CODES

CONTROL COMMANDS

NUM	*CODE*	*DEFINITION*	*KEYBOARD*	*HEX*
000	NUL	Null		00
001	SOH	Start of heading	CTRL-A	01
002	STX	Start text	CTRL-B	02
003	ETX	End text	CTRL-C	03
004	EOT	End of transmission	CTRL-D	04
005	ENQ	Enquiry	CTRL-E	05
006	ACK	Acknowledge	CTRL-F	06
007	BEL	Audible signal	CTRL-G	07
008	BS	Backspace	CTRL-H	08
009	HT	Horizontal tab	CTRL-I	09
010	LF	Line feed	CTRL-J	0A
011	VT	Vertical tab	CTRL-K	0B
012	FF	Form feed	CTRL-L	0C
013	CR	Carriage return	CTRL-M	0D
014	SO	Shift out	CTRL-N	0E
015	SI	Shift in	CTRL-O	0F
016	DLE	Data link escape	CTRL-P	10
017	DC1	Direct control 1	CTRL-Q	11
018	DC2	Direct control 2	CTRL-R	12
019	DC3	Direct control 3	CTRL-S	13
020	DC4	Direct control 4	CTRL-T	14
021	NAK	Negative acknowledge	CTRL-U	15

NUM	*CODE*	*DEFINITION*	*KEYBOARD*	*HEX*
022	SYN	Synchronous idle	CTRL-V	16
023	ETB	End transmission block	CTRL-W	17
024	CAN	Cancel	CTRL-X	18
025	EM	End of medium	CTRL-Y	19
026	SUB	Substitute	CTRL-Z	1A
027	ESC	Escape	CTRL-[	1B
028	FS	Forms separator	CTRL-\	1C
029	GS	Group separator	CTRL-]	1D
030	RS	Record separator	CTRL-^	1E
031	US	Unit separator	CTRL-_	1F
032	SP	Space		20

ASCII CODES

ASCII NUMBER CODES FOR CHARACTERS

NUMBERS		*LETTERS*				*SPECIAL CHARS.*	
Char	*Num*	*Char*	*Num*	*Char*	*Num*	*Char*	*Num*
0	048	A	065	a	097	!	033
1	049	B	066	b	098	"	034
2	050	C	067	c	099	#	035
3	051	D	068	d	100	$	036
4	052	E	069	e	101	%	037
5	053	F	070	f	102	&	038
6	054	G	071	g	103	'	039
7	055	H	072	h	104	(	040
8	056	I	073	i	105	)	041
9	057	J	074	j	106	*	042
		K	075	k	107	+	043
		L	076	l	108	,	044
		M	077	m	109	-	045
		N	078	n	110	.	046
		O	079	o	111	/	047
		P	080	p	112	:	058
		Q	081	q	113	;	059
		R	082	r	114	<	060
		S	083	s	115	=	061
		T	084	t	116	>	062
		U	085	u	117	?	063
		V	086	v	118	@	064
		W	087	w	119	[	091
		X	088	x	120	\	092
		Y	089	y	121	]	093
		Z	090	z	122	^	094
						–	095
						`	096
						{	123
						:	124
						}	125
						~	126
						DEL	127

Appendix B

NETWORKS

The services listed are only a sample. Contact the network for a complete listing. Times are local except where indicated. Fees and operating hours subject to change.

PHOTOGRAPHIC NETWORKS

PHOTO-1
150 Fifth Ave., New York, NY 10010

(212)929-8030

Services: Electronic Mail, Conferencing, Bulletin Board, Scheduling, Stock Photo Needs, Marketing for Photojournalists, Equipment, The Photographer's Phone Book, Trade Publication Articles, Press Credential Services.

Registration Fee: $100
Minimum Fee: None
Connect Time Fee: Prime time: $17. Non-prime time: $8.50
Operating Hours: 24 hours/day

PHOTONET
250 W. Fifty-seventh St., New York, NY 10019

(212)307-6999

Services: Electronic Mail, Bulletin Boards, Photonet Express Mail, Photo Agency Database, New Products, Stock and Assignment Requests, Mailing Lists, Equipment, Photonet Magazine, Trade Publications.

Registration Fee: $49
Minimum Fee: $24/month
Connect Time Fee: $24/hour at 300 bps; $48/hour at 1200 bps
Operating Hours: 24 hours/day, 7 days/week

OTHER NATIONAL NETWORKS

BRS/After Dark
1200 Route 7, Latham, NY 12110

(518)783-1161 (800)833-4707

Services: Electronic Mail, Bulletin Board, 25 Databases, Books in Print.

Registration Fee: $50
Minimum Fee: None
Connect Time Fee: $6-$20/hour. Charge varies according to database used.
Operating Hours: Mon.-Fri., 6 p.m.-4 a.m. Eastern; Sat. 6 a.m.-4 a.m. Eastern; Sun., 6 a.m.-2 p.m.

COMPUSERVE INFORMATION SERVICES
5000 Arlington Centre Blvd., Columbus OH 43220

(614)457-8600 (800)848-8199

Services: News, Weather, Sports, Movie Reviews, Periodicals, Electronic Mail, CB Simulation, Bulletin Board, Electronic Shopping, Electronic Banking, Clubs, Games and Entertainment, Grolier's Academic American Encyclopedia, Airline Guides, Travel Information, Business and Investment Information, Brokerage Services, Newsletters, Computing Software, Special Services for Professionals.

Registration Fee: $30 with one free hour
Minimum Fee: None
Connect Time Fee: Prime time: $22.50/hour at 300 bps; $35/hour at 1200 bps. Non-prime time: $6/hour at 300 bps; $17.50/hour at 1200 bps.
Operating Hours: Prime time: Mon.-Fri., 8 a.m.-6 p.m.; Non-prime time: Mon.-Fri., 6 p.m.-5 a.m.; Sat., Sun., holidays, 8 a.m.-5 a.m.

DELPHI
General Videotex Corporation
Three Blackstone St., Cambridge, MA 02139

(617)491-3393 (800)544-4005

Services: Appointment Calendar, Home Banking, Bulletin Board, Conferences, Games, Newsletter, Electronic Mail, News, Catalog Shopping, Travel, Typesetting Services, Research Library.

Registration Fee: $45.95
Minimum Fee: None
Connect Time Fee: Prime time: $11.50/hour at 300 bps. Non-prime time $5/hour at 300 bps.
Operating Hours: Prime time: Mon.-Fri., 8 a.m.-6 p.m. Non-prime time: Mon.-Fri., 6 p.m.-8 a.m.; Sat., Sun., holidays, 24 hours/day.

DOW JONES NEWS/RETRIEVAL SERVICE
P.O. Box 300, Princeton, NJ 08540

(609)452-2000 (800)257-5114

Services: Business and Economic News, Financial and Investment Services, Academic American Encyclopedia, News, Sports, Weather, Movie Reviews, Airline Guides.

Registration Fee: $50. Contact for package arrangements.
Minimum Fee: None
Connect Time Fee: Prime time: $36-$72/hour at 300 bps. Non-prime time: $9-$12/hour at 300 bps (1.7 times higher for 1200 bps)
Operating Hours: Prime time: Mon.-Fri., 6 a.m.-6 p.m.; Non-prime time: Mon.-Fri., 6 p.m.-4 a.m.; Sat., Sun., holidays, 6 a.m.-4 a.m.

KNOWLEDGE INDEX
Dialog Information Services, Inc.
Marketing Dept.
3460 Hillview Ave., Palo Alto, CA 94304

(415)858-3796 (800)227-5510

Services: News, Books in Print, Databases in Special Interest Areas.

Registration Fee: $35
Minimum Fee: None
Connect Time Fee: $24/hour
Operating Hours: Mon.-Thur., 6 p.m.-5 a.m.; Fri., 6 p.m.-midnight; Sat. 8 a.m.-midnight; Sun. 3 p.m.-5 a.m.

NEWSNET, INC.
Customer Service
945 Haverford Rd., Bryn Mawr, PA 19010

(215)527-8030 (in Pennsylvania) (800)345-1301

Services: Electronic Mail, Newsletters in many categories.

Registration Fee: None
Minimum Fee: $15/month
Connect Time Fee: Prime time: $24/hour at 300 bps; $48/hour at 1200. Non-prime time: $18/hour at 300 bps; $36/hour at 1200 bps. Does not include surcharge for reading newsletters. Surcharge varies with each letter.
Operating Hours: Prime time: Mon.-Fri., 8 a.m.-8 p.m.; Non-prime time: Mon.-Fri., 8 p.m.-8 a.m.; Sat., Sun., holidays, 24 hours/day.

THE SOURCE
1616 Anderson Rd., McLean, VA 22102

(703)734-7500 (800)336-3366 (800)572-2070 (in Virginia)

Services: News, Sports, Travel Guides, New York Restaurants, Political Commentary, Science and Technology, Business and Finance, Catalog Shopping, Education Courses, Electronic Mail, Software, Bulletin Board, Publications, Bulletin Board for Photography and Other Special Interest Groups.

Registration Fee: $100
Minimum Fee: $10/month
Connect Time Fee: Prime time: $20.75/hour at 300 bps; $25.75/hour at 1200 bps. Non-prime time $7.75/hour at 300 bps; $10.75/hour at 1200 bps. Plus 25 cents per connection.
Operating Hours: Prime time: Mon.-Fri., 7 a.m.-6 p.m. Non-prime time: Mon.-Fri., 6 p.m.-4 a.m.; Sat., Sun., holidays, 6 a.m.-4 a.m.

Appendix C

TOUR OF PHOTONET

The Photonet network is very easy to use. Just follow the on-line instructions. To sign on, you dial your local number. Once you have made a connection, proceed as follows: Photonet's messages appear on the left, cuing my responses, which appear to the right. What follows is a typical "day's work" on the system—letters received and sent, stock requests checked—all done in just 12 minutes. Note: ↑ indicates "RET" or "ENT" key. Photonet prompts you with a >. My comments are indicated by <.

ATDT277-7942	<Local Telephone Number
CONNECT	<Connection made
00000↑	<Enter 5 alphabetic O's.
CSS ON-LINE—LA2	<Message that you are on-line
>LINK NCS1↑	<Enter LINK NCS1.
>P1181↑	<Enter your Photonet number.
password:	
>PASSWORD↑	<Enter your password. Wait for mask to stop.
A/C INFO:	
>↑	<Enter "RET" or "ENT."
NCS1 READY AT 15.21.17 ON 30 OCT 84. CSS.304 15 JUN 82	
WELCOME TO PHOTONET!	

*** YOU HAVE 2 LETTERS ON FILE *** <I am told if I have letters waiting.

PAGE NUMBER OR <M>AIN MENU...
>M↑

When you first sign on to the system, enter "M" for main menu. Later on when you become more experienced with the system, you can go directly to the information you are interested in by entering its page number. Consult your Photonet User's Manual for the page numbers.

P00000 <Page number of main menu

PHOTONET MAIN DIRECTORY
----
1) COMMUNICATIONS
2) NEWS AND INFORMATION
3) PHOTOGRAPHIC AGENCIES
4) PHOTO RESEARCH DIRECTORY
5) THE MARKETPLACE
6) MFG. PROFESSIONAL SERVICES
7) EXIT PHOTONET

PLEASE ENTER YOUR SELECTION...
>1↑ <I enter "1" for "Communications."

From the master menu, you can select any one of the major areas you are interested in. Consult your User's Manual to find out what is under each major category. Selecting 7) EXIT PHOTONET will terminate your session on Photonet.

P10000 <Page number for communications menu

COMMUNICATIONS
----
1) ELECTRONIC MAIL
2) REGIONAL BULLETIN BOARDS

3) PHOTONET FEEDBACK
4) PHOTONET EXPRESS
5) RETURN TO PREVIOUS PAGE
PLEASE ENTER YOUR
SELECTION...
>1↑ <I select Electronic Mail.

Under "Communications," you can select one of the bulletin boards, send a letter via electronic mail or Photonet Express, or leave a message with Photonet.

P11000 <Page number for electronic mail

ELECTRONIC MAIL (PMAIL)
----
1) READ PMAIL
2) SEND PMAIL
3) RETURN TO PREVIOUS PAGE

PLEASE ENTER YOUR
SELECTION...
>1↑ <I select "1" to read my letters.

P11100 <Page number for reading mail

READ PMAIL

ONE MOMENT PLEASE, PROCESSING YOUR MAIL...

DO YOU WANT SPEED PROMPTS? Y/N
>N↑ <I answer "no" to speed prompts.

*** YOU HAVE 2 LETTERS ***

ENTER NUMBER OF LETTER YOU WISH TO READ, "L" TO LIST ALL LETTERS, OR "E" TO END...

>L↑ <I enter "L" to list letters.

DATE	FROM	SUBJECT	TIME
1. 10/26/84	P0321 – HARRY HAYES	PHOTO LEAD	22.31.50
2. 10/28/84	P0987 – KAY	DENVER TRIP	09.15.40

ENTER NUMBER OF LETTER YOU WISH TO READ, "L" TO LIST ALL LETTERS, OR "E" TO END...

>1↑ <This time I enter "1" to read my first letter.

10/26/84 P0321 – HARRY HAYES PHOTO LEAD 22.31.50

WELCOME BACK FROM YOUR TRIP TO ALBUQUERQUE. JUST IN TIME. UNION CALENDAR COMPANY IS DOING A SPECIAL CALENDAR ON HOT-AIR BALLOONS. YOU CAN CONTACT THEM ON PMAIL. THEIR NUMBER IS P0789.

PRESS "R" TO READ AGAIN, "F" TO FILE, "D" TO DELETE, "I" FOR INSTANT REPLY, OR "X" FOR INSTANT REPLY THEN DELETE...
>D↑ <I delete this letter.

ENTER NUMBER OF LETTER YOU WISH TO READ, "L" TO LIST ALL LETTERS, OR "E" TO END...
>2↑ <I enter the number of my second letter.

10/28/84 P0987 – KAY DENVER TRIP 09.15.40

I WILL BE IN DENVER ON THE 30TH. CAN YOU MEET ME THERE?

PRESS "R" TO READ AGAIN, "F" TO FILE, "D" TO DELETE, "I" FOR INSTANT REPLY, OR "X" FOR INSTANT REPLY THEN DELETE...
>X↑ <I enter "X" for instant reply.

Initially, you will want to answer "N" to speed prompts. Later on when you get used to the mailing procedure, you will want to use the shortened speed prompts so you can get through the mail process quickly.

P11200 <Page number for sending mail

SEND PMAIL
- - - - - - - - - - -
WOULD YOU LIKE SPEED PROMPTS? Y/N
>N↑

ENTER ID NUMBER OF THE PERSON YOU WISH TO RECEIVE THIS LETTER, OR PRESS "E" TO END ELECTRONIC MAIL...
>P0987↑ <Enter Photonet number of person.

THIS LETTER IS BEING SENT TO:
KAY BALLARD <Photonet verifies your number entry.

PRESS "ENTER" IF CORRECT, OR PRESS "C" TO CHANGE...
>↑ <Correct if name is not correct.

ENTER YOUR NAME (UP TO 20 LETTERS)...
>NADINE↑

YOU ENTERED: NADINE
PRESS "ENTER" IF CORRECT, OR PRESS "C" TO CHANGE...
>↑

ENTER SUBJECT (UP TO 25 LETTERS)...
>DENVER TRIP↑

YOU ENTERED: DENVER TRIP
PRESS "ENTER" IF CORRECT, OR PRESS "C" TO CHANGE...
>↑

ENTER YOUR LETTER. WHEN YOU HAVE FINISHED YOUR LETTER, GO TO THE NEXT LINE AND ENTER "XXXX"...

ENTER LINE 1...
>YES. CAN MEET YOU IN DENVER BUT I WON'T BE THERE UNTIL NOV 3.↑

ENTER LINE 2...
>XXXX↑ <XXXX ends letter.

WHAT WOULD YOU LIKE TO DO WITH THIS LETTER?
PRESS "R" TO REVIEW, PRESS "S" TO SEND, PRESS "D" TO DELETE...
>S↑ <I send letter.

LETTER SENT...

PRESS "S" TO SEND ANOTHER LETTER, OR PRESS "E" TO END ELECTRONIC MAIL...
>E↑ <I do not want to send more letters.

ONE MOMENT, PLEASE, PROCESSING PMAIL REQUESTS...

After the letter requests are completed, Photonet returns to the Electronic Mail Menu. You can do more letter processing, go back to the previous menu, or "jump" directly to the next section you want to use by entering the page number.

P11000

ELECTRONIC MAIL (PMAIL)
----
1) READ PMAIL
2) SEND PMAIL
3) RETURN TO PREVIOUS PAGE

PLEASE ENTER YOUR SELECTION...
>P40000↑ <I select the page number for the PHOTO RESEARCH DIRECTORY.

I have decided to go directly to the PHOTO RESEARCH DIRECTORY. Until you have learned the system, it will be easier for you to just work back through the menus.

P40000

PHOTO RESEARCH DIRECTORY
----
1) PLACE A PHOTO REQUEST
2) STOCK UPDATE—NEW IMAGES
3) TRAVEL UPDATE—ITINERARIES
4) SUBSCRIBER/PHOTO SOURCES DIRECTORY
5) STOCK PHOTOGRAPHY REQUESTS
6) ASSIGNMENT PHOTOGRAPHY REQUESTS
7) RETURN TO PREVIOUS PAGE

PLEASE ENTER YOUR SELECTION...
>5↑ <I select STOCK PHOTOGRAPHY REQUESTS.

P45000 <Page number for Stock Photo Requests

STOCK PHOTOGRAPHY REQUESTS
----
1) 0372 HORSE CART 2) 0388 RECRUIT PHOTOGS
3) 0390 MURPHY HOTEL 4) 0409 LASERS
5) 0416 VIDEODISC PHOTOS 6) 0418 MALI, GR. BRIT.
7) 0421 500 SUBJECTS 8) 0425 HANDICAPPED

9) 0437 VERONA, ITALY
10) 0438 CHRISTMAS
11) 0445 IND ROBOTICS
12) 0449 CITY LIGHTS
13) 0450 SUNROOM
14) 0454 GAMBLING
15) 0455 TEXTILES
16) 0456 BELGIUM
17) 0457 NEW ORLEANS
18) 0458 "5"
19) 0466 FOSSILS
20) 0467 WITCH HAZEL
21) 0468 BURRS
22) 0469 FOOD
23) 0470 ANIMALS

ENTER NUMBER OF REQUEST YOU WISH TO READ,
"L" TO LIST ALL REQUESTS, "E" TO END...
>23↑ <I select "23—ANIMALS."

0470 ANIMALS 10/04/84 19.41.56 POSTED BY: P0112

NEED THE FOLLOWING ANIMALS FOR A CHILDREN'S ENCYCLOPEDIA. LION, ASIAN...TIGER, BENGAL...SQUIRREL, FLYING...PYTHON, GREEN TREE...KANGAROO, GREAT GRAY...HORSE, ASIATIC WILD... CONDOR, CALIFORNIA...RHINOCEROS, INDIAN...EAGLE, MONKEY-EATING...CAT, PALLAS...

CONTACT IMMEDIATELY BY PMAIL OR CALL AT (793) 945-0987.

PRESS "ENTER" TO CONTINUE...
>↑

ENTER NUMBER OF REQUEST YOU WISH TO READ,
"L" TO LIST ALL REQUESTS, "E" TO END...
>E↑

The system returns to the previous menu. You can quit Photonet by returning back to the main menu and selecting 7) EXIT PHOTONET or by entering PBYE.

P40000

PHOTO RESEARCH DIRECTORY
----
1) PLACE A PHOTO REQUEST
2) STOCK UPDATE—NEW IMAGES
3) TRAVEL UPDATE—ITINERARIES
4) SUBSCRIBER/PHOTO SOURCES DIRECTORY
5) STOCK PHOTOGRAPHY REQUESTS
6) ASSIGNMENT PHOTOGRAPHY REQUESTS
7) RETURN TO PREVIOUS PAGE

```
PLEASE ENTER YOUR SELECTION...
>PBYE↑                              <I sign off.

PBYE

THANK YOU FOR USING PHOTONET!

3.41 ARU'S, .20 CONNECT HRS        <Connect time 12 minutes
LOGGED OFF AT 15.33.00 ON 30 OCT 84
NO CARRIER                          <Disconnected
```

At the end of your session, Photonet gives you the time you were on the system in increments of $^{1}/_{100}$ths of an hour.

Glossary

access: The ability to obtain data from a storage device and make it available in the computer's memory.

acoustic coupler: Part of a modem used for receiving and transmitting data using a telephone handset. See *modem.*

all-in-one computer: A computer consisting of a central processing unit, memory, input/output interfaces, disk drives, monitor, and keyboard—all in the same housing.

alphanumeric: A contraction of *alphabetics* and *numerics.* Characters are letters, numbers, punctuation, and special characters.

applications software: Programs designed to handle specific types of information, such as accounting.

ASCII: American Standard Code for Information Interchange. A binary coding system used to represent letters, numbers, special characters, and commands.

assembly language: A low-level programming language that replaces machine language binary codes with symbolic instructions. An assembler translates these symbols back into machine language.

asynchronous transmission: Data communications in which the beginning and end of a character is signaled by start and stop bits. See *synchronous transmission.*

backup: A copy of information to provide security, should the original become unusable.

BASIC: Beginner's All-purpose Symbolic Instruction Code. An easy-to-learn, high-level programming language that is popular with microcomputer users.

baud: A unit for measuring data transmission speeds over a communications line. *Baud* and *bit* are used interchangeably, although technically they are not precisely the same. The baud rate in microcomputer systems is usually either 300 or 1200 bauds per second.

Bell compatible: A term used to describe modems that meet the industry standard established by Bell Telephone system modems.

binary: A number system based on the powers of two. Numbers are expressed as *0* and *1* and are referred to as binary digits.

bit: Contraction for *binary digit.*

boot: Loading the operating system into the computer's memory.

briefcase computer: A computer that is similar to a briefcase in size and shape. A medium-size portable computer.

bubble memory: A form of data storage where bits are represented on magnetized "bubbles."

buffer: An area of the computer memory where data can be temporarily stored until it is moved to permanent storage.

bug: An error or default in a program.

bundled: A package deal in which the software is included in the price of the hardware.

byte: A group of eight bits that represent one character of information.

canned software: Packaged software general enough to be used by many users.

cathode-ray tube: A video display that is used in television sets and computer monitors.

CBBS: Computerized Bulletin Board Service.

central processing unit: The "brain" of the computer that contains the arithmetic, logic, and control sections that interpret and carry out instructions.

character: A letter, number, punctuation mark, or special symbol. Synonymous with *byte.*

chip: An integrated circuit. Microscopic circuits etched on a small sliver of silicon.

code: Symbolic characters used to represent data.

compiler: A program that translates high-level language program instructions (source program) into machine-language instructions (object code).

computer: A machine that processes information. Digital computers process precise information in the form of discrete bits.

configuration: The layout or design of elements in a hardware or data processing system.

connect time: The time during which a communications link is established. Usually used as a basis of billing on an on-line network and measured in fractions of an hour.

copy: To transfer data from one file to another, making a duplicate file.

CP/M: Control Program/Microcomputer. A popular operating system for 8-bit computers.

CPU: Central Processing Unit.
CRT: Cathode-ray tube.
cursor: A movable indicator on the screen of a video monitor.
custom software: Programs designed for a specific user's requirements.
data: Information that is put into a computer.
database: A file containing information on a particular subject.
data base management system (DBMS): A complex software system that controls a data base.
data communications: Transferring data from one computer to another by a transmission system such as telephone lines.
data processing: The manipulation of information, using a computer.
default: A value that is automatically assigned if another is not specified.
demodulate: Converts voice-grade signals of a communications line into digital bits. See *modulation.*
density: The amount of information stored in a physical area of a disk.
DIP switches: Duel In-line Package. On/off switches that allow the user to select certain options without hardware alterations.
directory: A file containing the names and locations of all the files contained on the disk.
disk: A data storage device that resembles a phonograph record. Special disks used in microcomputers are called floppy disks or diskettes.
documentation: All information about a computer or software. Can include operating instructions, programs, servicing information, and so on.
dot matrix: The formation of characters by arranging dots into a grid pattern.
double-density: The ability to write twice as much data in a given area on a disk.
double-sided: Disks and disk drives that can record information on both sides of the disk.
download: Capturing data transmissions from another computer.
dual processor: A computer with two microprocessors.
dumb terminal: A terminal not controlled by its own microprocessor.
edit: To check and correct errors.
electronic mail: A method of transmitting correspondence and other communications over telephone lines using computers.
erase: To remove all reference to a file from the disk directory.
error message: A message displayed by software when it has encountered a problem or error in the data.
execute: To perform an operation.
field: One item of information in a record, such as a name.

file: A collection of related information or records.

file name extension: The second part of the file name, separated from the main file name by a period.

firmware: A program that has been permanently stored in read-only memory (ROM).

full-duplex: Data communications mode wherein signals are sent and received simultaneously.

function keys: Special keys that are programmed to perform a command.

half-duplex: Data communications mode where signals are sent in only one direction at a time.

hand-held computer: A small, battery-powered computer that can be held in one hand.

handshaking: Exchange of signals between two computers prior to data communications.

hard copy: Computer output printed on paper.

hard disk: High-capacity, fast-access disk.

hardware: The physical components of a computer system.

help: Information directly available in a system that explains how it works.

high-level programming language: English-language-type programming language.

housekeeping: Activities designed to keep the system functioning in an orderly manner.

implementation: The process of installing and testing new pieces of hardware and software.

input: Data entered into a computer system.

integrated circuits: Electronic circuits that are microscopically etched on a semiconductor. Often called *chips*.

interface: A point where two components of a computer system come together.

interpreter: A program that translates high-level program language instructions (source code) into binary machine code (object code), but the translation and execution of the code is done one statement at a time.

K: Kilo, meaning thousand. 1K = 1024. Usually used to describe computer memory size.

key: A field or fields within a record used to uniquely identify the record. Also, a button on a keyboard.

keypad: A cluster of special-purpose keys on a keyboard.

large scale integration (LSI): The process used to make integrated circuits or chips.

LCD: Liquid-Crystal Display. The display used in digital watches and in pocket and briefcase computers.

M: Mega, meaning million. 1M = 1,048,576 bytes. Often referred to as a Meg. Used to describe hard-disk storage and large-capacity memory.

machine language: The binary language used by a computer.

mainframe: A very large computer.

memory: Data storage area in a computer. See RAM and ROM.

menu: A list of choices displayed by a computer program. The user selects the option he wants.

microcomputer: A small, inexpensive computer.

microprocessor: A small central processing unit contained on a chip.

minicomputer: A small- to medium-sized computer between a microcomputer and a mainframe. It is getting difficult to distinguish between a mini- and a microcomputer. Generally, a minicomputer has greater storage capacity and supports multiple users.

modem: MOdulator/DEModulator. A device that translates the digital signals of a computer into the voice-grade signals of a telephone line and back again.

modulation: Convert digital bits of a computer into the voice-grade signals of a communication line.

monitor: A screen which allows the computer to display information.

multi-user system: A computer system where more than one person can use the system at the same time.

network: A group of computers or terminals interconnected by telephone or other communication lines. Also, a service for distribution of information to subscribers.

object code: Machine-language binary code.

on-line: A terminal device is on-line when it is in communication with and under the control of a computer.

operating system: A program that controls all other software and performs functions necessary to the system operation.

output: The result of data processing activity.

overprinting: Printing over previously printed characters to improve the type or emphasize the character.

parallel test: A method of testing new software where both the old and the new system process the same data. The results are compared to verify the accuracy of the new system.

parallel transmission: Data transmission where all bits in a byte are transmitted simultaneously.

parity check: A method of checking the accuracy of transmitted data. An extra parity bit is included with each character to make the sum of the bits either even or odd, depending on the agreed-upon convention.

password: A security method to restrict access to data. A special code word is needed before information can be accessed.

peripheral: Any input/output hardware device connected to a computer. Includes such things as printers, disk drives, modems, etc.

personal computer: A moderately priced microcomputer designed for a single user for use in the home or small business environment.

phoneme: The smallest component of speech.

pixel: The smallest picture element on a video display.

portable computer: A computer that can be conveniently hand carried.

printer: An output device that produces computer output in readable form on paper.

program: Instructions given to a computer to make it perform a special task. Also referred to as software.

programmer: A person who codes instructions into a form that can be used by a computer.

prompt: A message generated by the software to instruct the user to input certain data.

protocol: The rules for communication between two computers.

RAM: Random-Access Memory.

Random-Access Memory (RAM): Computer storage that is directly accessible by the CPU; allows information to be written into it and read from it. Information in RAM is not retained when the power is shut off.

Read-Only Memory (ROM): Computer storage in the form of solid state integrated circuits that stores permanent data and is not lost when the power supply is turned off. The data cannot be changed.

record: A group of related data. Individual records make up a file. Individual information elements within a record are referred to as fields.

report: A printed document produced by a computer as the result of some data processing.

ROM: Read-Only Memory.

RS-232(RS-232-C): A standard connector used to interface computers with serial peripheral devices.

scrolling: Movement of text vertically or horizontally on a screen monitor so that portions of the text that cannot fit on the screen can be brought into view.

sectors: Areas on a disk where data are stored.

semiconductor: A material which services as an electronic conductor in integrated circuits. The most commonly used substance is silicon.

serial transmission: The transmission of a byte one bit at a time. See *parallel transmission*.

sign-off: A command on a terminal that ends the transmission on a network.

sign-on: A command on a terminal that initiates a session on a network.

software: Instructions that tell a computer what to do.

sort: To arrange data or records in a specified order.

source code: Statements in a computer program.

speech synthesizer: A device that enables a computer to mimic speech by using phonemes.

spelling checker: Proofreading software that compares the words of text to words in a dictionary and indicates words that have no match.

split screen: The software divides the screen so that two different files or different portions of the same file can be viewed on the screen simultaneously.

spreadsheet: Software that simulates an accounting worksheet.

storage device: A computer peripheral capable of holding programs and data more or less permanently; can be accessed by a computer. Disks are the common medium of storage in small computers.

surge protector: A device that plugs into a wall socket and prevents surges and spikes in the electric current from reaching the computer and causing possible damage.

synchronous transmission: Character transmission is controlled by a clocking device that determines the beginning and end of a character.

SYSGEN: SYStem GENeration. Initializing and generating an operating system.

sysop: SYStem OPerator. A person who operates a bulletin board.

systems analyst: A person who defines activities to best accomplish certain operations, usually in terms of a computer environment.

tag: A name attached to an item for identification purposes.

telecommunications: Any transmission between two devices, usually via telephone lines.

terminal: Any input or output device connected to a computer that is capable of sending or receiving information from the computer.

time sharing: An installation where several users can utilize the facilities of a large computer at the same time.

track: The organization of a disk into concentric circles.

tutorial: Instructional example of how to run a particular piece of software.

upload: To send a file over telephone lines to another computer.

user: A person who uses a computer system.

user-friendly: Refers to software or hardware that is easy for an inexperienced person to use without special training.

user group: A group of people who share information about a computer or software through meetings or publications.

verify: To check the accuracy of data.

voice recognition: A system that accepts spoken words as input commands.

Winchester disk: A hard-disk system packaged in airtight housing. Especially developed for a small computer environment.

word processing: A computer program for writing, editing, revising, formatting, and printing text.

write-protect: A procedure used to prevent accidental writing of material on a disk.

Index

About the Author

B. Nadine Orabona, a graduate of the School of Modern Photography, is a freelance photographer who specializes in animal and nature photography. She is also a professional computer consultant with seventeen years' experience in the analysis, design, and implementation of data processing systems for business.

When Orabona needed to find a way to use her personal computer to simplify her photography business details, these two areas of expertise came together, and the results were so successful that she was urged to share them with other photographers.

Her photographs have been published in such magazines as *National Wildlife, International Wildlife, Animal Kingdom,* and *Flight;* she has had two articles published in Petersen's *PhotoGraphic* magazine; and she has two new books currently in the works—one on wildlife photography and the other a photographer's guide to California. Her photographic awards include Grand Prize in the Century City Photographic Contest in 1978, Best Nature Picture of 1980 from the Southern California Council of Camera Clubs, and two bronze medals (one for color, one for nature) in 1980 from the Camera Circle of Glendale. She lives in Southern California.

OTHER WRITER'S DIGEST BOOKS OF INTEREST

BRITISH JOURNAL OF PHOTOGRAPHY ANNUAL—This outstanding yearbook contains more than 150 color and black and white photos, articles on techniques and current trends, and a section filled with chemical formulae for mixing processing solutions. 9¾x10¼, 222 pages, $24.95

DEVELOPING THE CREATIVE EDGE IN PHOTOGRAPHY, by Bert Eifer—How to turn average pictures into stunning photographs using Eifer's creative techniques. 8x8, 208 pages, 40 color pages, b&w illus. throughout, $16.95 (paper)

HOW TO CREATE AND SELL PHOTO PRODUCTS, by Mike and Carol Werner—Over 30 sets of instructions for making and selling products featuring your photos, including clocks, greeting cards, calendars, lamp shades, and more. 380 pages, 100 b&w photos, $14.95 (paper)

HOW TO CREATE SUPER SLIDE SHOWS, by E. Burt Close—Whether for family and friends or for profit, here's how to put on a show that will turn yawns into applause. 220 pages, $10.95 (paper)

HOW YOU CAN MAKE $25,000 A YEAR WITH YOUR CAMERA (NO MATTER WHERE YOU LIVE), by Larry Cribb—scores of profitable jobs for freelance photographers available right in your own community, with details on how to find and get the job, equipment, what to charge. 194 pages, $9.95 (paper)

PHOTOGRAPHER'S MARKET—This annual directory lists 2,500 photo buyers—stock photo agencies, periodicals, ad agencies, book publishers, and galleries, complete with full contact details. 6x9, 576 pages, $15.95

SELL & RE-SELL YOUR PHOTOS, by Rohn Engh—Takes you step by step through the process of selling your photos by mail, using the right techniques for each market. Plus advice on taxes, record-keeping, marketing and sales tips. 323 pages, 40 b&w photos, $14.95

STARTING AND SUCCEEDING IN YOUR OWN PHOTOGRAPHY BUSINESS, by Jeanne Thwaites—A no-nonsense guide for starting your own photography studio, including how to choose a location, select equipment, advertise, manage finances and more. 343 pages, b&w illus. $18.95

WILDLIFE & NATURE PHOTOGRAPHER'S FIELD GUIDE, by Michael Freeman—A compact guide filled with striking photos, practical tips, and photography instruction. 224 pages, 90 color photos, $14.95